NAHC

Wild Game
Cookbook

designed and edited by

Mike Vail
Bill Miller

Published by the ~~North American Hunting Club~~, Inc.
Minneapolis, Minnesota

We would like to thank the following for their help:

Larry Anderson, for the beautiful wildlife drawings which enhance this *NAHC Wild Game Cookbook*.

4-H Shooting Program, for their delicious recipes and helpful kitchen hints.

Browning Firearms, for the use of the cover photograph.

Bob & Matt Allen, **The Buck Family**, and **Roy & Ed Weatherby** for sharing their families' hunting stories.

Hunting Celebrities, for allowing us to share their favorite game recipes.

Members of the North American Hunting Club, for the recipes they submitted and their support through the first ten years of the North American Hunting Club.

Cover photo courtesy of Browning, Route 1, Morgan, Utah 85040.

Address reprint requests and orders for additional books to:

NAHC Cookbook Editor
PO Box 35557
Minneapolis, MN 55435

Library of Congress Catalog Card Number 84-649847
ISBN 0-914697-13-7
Copyright 1987, North American Hunting Club, Inc.

CONTENTS

NAHC Enhancing Hunting Skills And Enjoyment For 10 Years

"You shot it, you clean it!"

That's almost a universal law governing the relationship between modern hunter and family when it comes to preparing game for the kitchen. But it hasn't always been so.

Even today, among Eskimos and other groups that still rely on hunting for subsistence, the work resulting from a successful hunt is passed from the men to the women and children once the game is brought into the village. Wild meat care and cooking among these people are life or death skills passed from adults to children, generation to generation.

To us and to the future of hunting, passing on the traditions of our sport has the same degree of life and death importance. All of hunting and all of the tradition we love is in the balance. If we do not share with today's youth the excitement we feel every time we hear a bull elk bugle, a turkey gobble or a mallard taking flight, then the sport of hunting will never survive. If we do not guide young hunters in proper safety technique and hunting ethics, anti-hunting factions will quickly close the door on all hunting opportunities.

As the North American Hunting Club celebrates its 10th anniversary during 1988, we are rededicating the Club and this *Wild Game Cookbook* to the NAHC's most basic goal of enhancing the hunting skills and enjoyment of veteran and novice hunters alike.

In 10 short years we've done a great deal toward that end, and in the years to come, with continued growth and the help of dedicated members, such as you, we'll be able to do even more.

The seed of the North American Hunting Club was planted 50 years ago in a boy hunting squirrels and pheasants on his grandfather's farm in southern Minnesota. That's where NAHC Chairman of the Board, Paul Burke, acquired his passion for hunting. By the time I entered the Marine Corps in 1974, Paul and I had made numerous trips to hunt big and small game across the continent.

It doesn't seem possible that it was already 10 years ago when Paul, my father, tossed the outdoor magazine he was reading on the end table in his Minneapolis-area home. Disenchanted with useless stories like "How to Disassemble an Antique Three-barreled European Shotgun," he thought, "Why can't I find a magazine that's just for hunters, one filled with hunting stories? I don't like to weed through crappie fishing articles or waste my time with maintenance reports about unusual guns."

As a hunter, Paul asked himself, "What else would I like to see in a magazine; what kind of information would help me enjoy hunting more? I know I would like to meet other hunters like myself, to share stories, experiences and possibly even hunting spots. I'd want to know what guides or outfitters they hunted with and whether they thought it would be worth my money to go with a particular outfitter.

"Likewise, I would like to know about the equipment other hunters are using and if they think it would be wise for me to invest in them or save my money for more reliable products. It also would be nice to buy hunting equipment at low prices, kind of like when I go into a sporting goods store and buy a case of shotgun shells with some hunting buddies.

"I would also like to compare my trophies with those taken by other hunters of my caliber. It would give me a little more incentive and enjoyment."

Paul shared these ideas with his closest hunting friends, and they agreed they were looking for such services too, but couldn't find one organization or group that provided them. Paul strongly believed that other hunters across the country felt the same way.

The same day I decided to accept my next three year assignment as a Marine Corps First Lieutenant, Paul called and said we were going to start the North American Hunting Club. It took a little finagling, but things worked out, and within a few months, I was on the way home from Okinawa, Japan.

Early response to the club was 1,500 members. It quickly grew to 15,000, then 30,000. Now, 10 years after the seed was planted, the North American Hunting Club has more than 150,000 members! And it continues to grow!

As NAHC members, you know about the valuable services our club offers. You know about and have read *North American Hunter*, the official publication of the North American Hunting Club. What you may not realize is that in its very first issues, *North American Hunter* started as a quarterly publication, and ran as one until September, 1980 before changing to its present bi-monthly format.

You also know about *Keeping Track* the member newsletter which includes Hunting Reports, Swap Hunts, Bits & Pieces and other important member services. These services are open to each and every member of the NAHC, and you are encouraged to use them often.

The Hunting Reports are evaluations of guides and outfitters with whom NAHC members have hunted. When a member returns from a guided hunt, he rates in his own words such things as quantity of game hunted, food, condition of camp equipment, experience of guide and other things you need to know before investing in a hunt with that guide or outfitter.

There are thousands of these reports submitted by your fellow NAHC members every year, so NAHC members like you who are planning a hunt know that the chances are good that a particular guide or outfitter they are considering has been rated by a fellow member.

The Swap Hunts benefit has been almost as popular as the Hunting Reports. They provide a way for you and your fellow members from across the country to meet and share hunting adventures . One member even has a goal of hosting at least one member from all 50 states in his Pennsylvania deer camp!

In the Discounts section NAHC members who own a business or provide valuable hunting services offer fellow NAHC members their wares at reduced prices. The NAHC can also save you money by ordering firearms and other hunting products for you directly from manufacturers and distributors.

Member Shots provide members an opportunity to share their trophies with other members of the Club. The best photos of members with their trophy animals of all species appear in each issue of *North American Hunter*. This gives all members the opportunity to compare their hunting success with their peers across North America.

Through the Club's Field Test Program, members receive new and valuable hunting equipment to try. When finished, they submit a report for other members to evaluate. These items, which range from buck scent or lures to shotguns and compound bows, are donated by various manufacturers. Members involved in the testing keep the item they receive.

Meeting Place is for members who would like to find new hunting partners in a specific area or state. It is especially

popular with members who move to a new region and would like to find some new hunting companions.

The NAHC also has an awards program honoring the members who take the largest trophies based on the Boone & Crockett scoring system during the scoring period. Every other year, a big game registry lists the top trophies taken with modern rifles, handguns, muzzleloaders and archery equipment. Annually, members who take the best trophy in each category win awards honoring their achievement.

Additionally, the most outstanding hunt each year will earn a deserving member the President's Trophy, the NAHC's highest honor recognizing member hunting prowess.

Another benefit that thousands of NAHC members take advantage of is the opportunity to win or earn free hunts during the annual membership drive contest. Every year thousands of dollars worth of hunts are given away! To win, all you have to do is encourage your friends and hunting partners to sign up for the NAHC. For example Life Member Tom Frame of Bridgeport, West Virginia, won a six-day black bear hunt in Idaho with Clearwater Outfitters in the 1986 random drawing, and he signed up only one new member!

Leased land is another reason many NAHC members join the Club. All of the NAHC leases are great places to hunt. And they are open to every NAHC member! About the only time they are booked up is the first few days of each state's respective firearms deer season.

So now, what will the next 10 years bring?

Growth. The stronger and larger the NAHC becomes, the more services we can provide. In the future we will have hundreds of swap hunt offerings, more products to field test, the most complete outfitter and guide rating service in the country, more great discounts on more hunting equipment, more leased land to hunt, and the best, most read hunting magazine in North America.

The future does look bright!

During the next 10 years and beyond, we'll all be looking for our children to support and carry on the traditions that

NAHC members have laid. The NAHC has wholeheartedly thrown its support and dollars behind the efforts of organizations like the Wildlife Legislative Fund Of America, the National Shooting Sports Foundation, Bowhunters Who Care, the National Bowhunter Education Foundation, the Outstanding American Handgunner Awards Foundation, the National Muzzleloading Rifle Association, and Ducks Unlimited among others. These efforts will, in the long run, ensure that the traditions like "you shot it, you clean it" will not die.

The results of those efforts can already be seen. The unsolicited photo and letter which follows was recently sent by NAHC member Mike Schroeder of Rice Lake, Wisconsin. In these few words from a proud father are revealed the reasons why we teach our children to hunt.

Enjoy it. Enjoy the stories and recipes in this book. And enjoy your time afield with sons and daughters.

In the expression of excitement on Nicole Schroeder's face, NAHC members can read all the reasons why we teach our children to hunt. Nicole took her beautiful 10-point whitetail on the opening day of Wisconsin's 1986 firearm deer season.

Dear NAHC,

The enclosed picture is that of my daughter, Nicole, who was 13 years old when this was taken (opening day Wisconsin rifle season 1986). She used an H&R .44 Magnum and 4 power scope to bag this beautiful 10-pointer just out of Millston, Wisconsin.

The reason I had to write was that each time I look at the picture, it not only brings back good memories, but it portrays to me what sport hunting is to be.

I not only see in her eyes the excitement of her first buck but I see also a pride in an accomplishment. I remember the enjoyment of the out-of-doors and the hunt. More realistically, as a hunter safety instructor, I see a hunt safely done. The biggest compliment to her was not this magnificent animal, but being invited to hunt with non-family members who stated a recognition of her awareness of the woods and firearm safety.

The vital thing I see is also a picture of the future for

hunting or shooting sports in general. I see a young person, like many others I have been privileged to meet, who is capable of representing the hunting fraternity by proper actions and reputation. I see in this picture a sportsman by the definition of the word.

I felt that I had to express these feelings somehow and thank you for listening.

Sincerely,
Mike Schroeder
Rice Lake, WI

Young hunter's recipes

ANDERSON...

The 4-H Shooting Sports/Wildlife Program

As a worldwide organization, the mission of 4-H is to assist youth in acquiring knowledge, developing life skills and forming attitudes which will enable them to become self-directing, productive and contributing members of society.

Familiar to most folks are agricultural related 4-H programs, but today, 4-H has moved into a wide cross section of interest areas geared for rural, suburban and urban youth alike. In Minnesota, one such project area is the Shooting Sports/Wildlife Program.

Minnesota 4-H Shooting Sports/Wildlife began in 1979 from 13 counties with 26 adult volunteer leaders and 350 youth members. Presently, all counties in Minnesota have a 4-H Shooting Sports/Wildlife project with over 3,500 youth and 900 leaders enrolled in the program.

It is from this pool of ambitious young outdoor enthusiasts that the recipes in this chapter have been collected. Not only are these recipes delicious, but they also represent an awareness amongst these 4-Hers of the importance of proper care and preparation of the game we take each season.

The Shooting Sports/Wildlife objective is to give young people the opportunity to experience and appreciate the recreational potential of shooting sports. Goals include:

1) develop leadership and citizenship qualities in youth.

2) promote an understanding of safe and responsible use of firearms.

3) develop and encourage a positive youth/adult relationship—particularly among family members.

4) develop self-discipline in skills.

5) learn sportsmanship and ethical behavior.

6) develop an appreciation for history and tradition of shooting sports.

7) appreciate shooting sports as a lifetime recreation or career.

8) develop an understanding of the principles of wildlife management.

These goals are accomplished through a wide range of activities which teach the basics of conservation, shooting disciplines and much much more.

The ultimate goal of the Shooting Sports and Wildlife Project is not the training of highly skilled, competitive shooters, but rather, the training of young people. Shooting is used as a medium for this training. In the process of working with their gun or bow, a youngster will meet with challenges, responsibilities, successes and failures which will certainly help him or her grow as a person.

For more information on the 4-H Shooting Sports, contact:
Agricultural Extension Service
4-H Youth Development
340 Coffey Hall
1420 Eckles Avenue
St. Paul, Minnesota 55108

TABLE OF WEIGHTS & MEASURES

MEASUREMENT CONVERSIONS

1 pinch = less than ⅛ tsp.
1 tbsp. = 3 tsp.
2 tbsp. = 1 oz.
4 tbsp. = ¼ cup
5 tbsp. + 1 tsp. = ⅓ cup
8 tbsp. = ½ cup
10 tbsp. + 2 tsp. = ⅔ cup
12 tbsp. = ¾ cup
16 tbsp. = 1 cup

1 cup = 8 oz.
1 pint = 16 oz.
1 quart = 32 oz.
1 gallon = 128 oz.

1 cup = ½ pint
2 cups = 1 pint
4 cups = 1 quart
2 pints = 1 quart
4 pints = ½ gallon
8 pints = 1 gallon
4 quarts = 1 gallon
8 gallons = 1 bushel

OVEN TEMPEATURES

Very Slow	225 to 250 Degrees
Slow	250 to 300 Degrees
Moderate	300 to 350 Degrees
Moderately Hot	350 to 400 Degrees
Hot	400 to 450 Degrees
Very Hot	450 to 500 Degrees

CAN SIZES

Number 1 =	16 oz. =	2 cups
Number 2 =	20 oz. =	2½ cups
Number 2½ =	28 oz. =	3½ cups
Number 3 =	32 oz. =	4 cups
Number 10 =	104 oz. =	13 cups
Number 300 =	14 oz. =	1¾ cups
Number 303 =	16 oz. =	2 cups

Chicken Fried Venison Steak

Serves: 2
Prep Time: 5 hours

1-2 **lbs. venison steaks**
  1 **egg**
  2 **cups milk**
    creole seasonings to taste
    cooking oil
    flour
    milk

Hammer steaks to tenderize and add seasonings. Beat milk and eggs. Marinate meat in mixture for 3 to 4 hours. Put ¼ to ⅜-inch cooking oil in skillet and heat. When oil is very hot, remove steaks from marinade, dredge in flour and place in skillet. Brown on each side. Do not over cook. Pour off oil, add milk. In separate container, mix flour, salt, pepper and milk for gravy base. Add to meat, cook and stir until gravy thickens.

Andrew Stevens
Loganberries 4-H

Venison Jerky

Serves: several
Prep Time: 12 hours

> 2 **lbs. venison**
> ½ **cup soy sauce**
> ½ **tsp. garlic powder**
> 1 **tsp. grated lemon peel**
> ¼ **tsp. pepper**

Cut venison into ¼-inch strips. Remove all fat. Mix all other ingredients. Dip venison into sauce and lay strips on baking sheet. Dry in oven or over wood stove for 10 to 12 hours at 150 to 175 degrees.

George Haberman
Anoka County 4-H

Venison Sloppy Joes

Serves: 8-10
Prep Time: ½ hour

> 2 **lbs. ground venison**
> 1 **lb. ground beef**
> 1 **med. onion, chopped**
> 1 **stem celery, finely sliced**
> 1 **tsp. garlic, chopped**
> 1 **can tomato soup**
> 1½ **cups V-8 juice**

Brown meat and chopped vegetables. Drain off excess fat. Add soup and V-8 juice and mix well. Heat. Serve on buns.

Bonnie Dircks
Anoka County 4-H

Norwegian Meatballs

Serves: 4
Prep Time: 1 hour

1½ **lbs. ground venison**
 ½ **cup breadcrumbs**
 2 **T. butter**
 ⅓ **cup onion, chopped**
 ½ **cup milk**
   salt
 ⅛ **tsp. nutmeg**
 ⅛ **tsp. allspice**
 ¼ **tsp. pepper**
 1 **tsp. sugar**
 1 **egg**
 3 **T. flour**
 2 **cups liquid (milk or water)**

Saute onions in butter until transparent. Mix meat, onions, breadcrumbs and egg, beat in milk, sugar, nutmeg, salt and allspice. Shape into 1-inch balls. Brown meatballs in skillet. Remove and keep warm. Blend flour, salt and liquid and add to skillet. Heat until bubbly. Meatballs can be simmered in gravy if desired.

Todd Brown
Loganberries 4-H

Venison Chili

Serves: 6
Prep Time: 2 hours

- **3 cups venison, cubed**
- **½ bunch celery, chopped**
- **2 lg. onions, cubed**
- **1 14 oz. bottle catsup**
- **1 15 oz. can whole tomatoes**
- **1 15 oz. can pork and beans or kidney beans**
- **2 cups water**
- **1 T. chili powder**
- **1 tsp. pepper**
- **1 tsp. paprika**
- **1 T. brown sugar**
- **2 cloves garlic, chopped**
- **2 T. butter**

Saute onions, garlic, celery, paprika and chili powder in butter. Add venison cubes. Stir until meat is well coated. Pour in catsup and tomatoes. Stir until well blended. Bring to a boil. Add water and cook for 20 minutes. Season with salt, pepper and brown sugar. Add beans and simmer for 1 hour.

Tammy Lynn Haakonson
Benton County 4-H

Venison Chops in Sour Cream

Serves: 6
Prep Time: 45 minutes

  6 **venison chops, ½-inch thick**
  ½ **tsp. powdered sage**
  ½ **tsp. salt**
      dash of pepper
  2 **T. shortening**
  2 **onions, sliced**
  1 **beef bouillon cube**
  ¼ **cup boiling water**
  ½ **cup sour cream**
  1 **T. flour**
  1 **T. parsley flakes, crushed**

Rub chops with mixture of sage, salt and pepper. Brown in shortening. Drain off extra fat. Add onion. Dissolve bouillon cube in hot water, pour over chops. Cover skillet, simmer for 25 to 30 minutes until meat is done. Remove meat to hot platter. Combine sour cream and flour in a bowl. Slowly stir mixture into drippings until mixed well. Return gravy to skillet and boil. Add a little water to thin gravy. Pour over chops. Sprinkle with parsley flakes. Can be served with noodles.

Jason Erickson
Lamplighters 4-H

Sausage Stuffed Mushrooms

Serves: several
Prep Time: 1 hour

1½ lbs. med. mushrooms
½ lb. ground venison sausage
½ cup shredded mozzarella cheese
¼ cup breadcrumbs
parsley

Preheat oven to 450 degrees. Remove stems from mushrooms and chop. Put caps aside. Cook sausage in skillet until brown. Remove and drain on towel. Save 2 T. drippings. Cook diced mushroom stems in drippings for 10 minutes. Remove skillet from stove, stir in sausage, cheese and breadcrumbs. Fill mushroom caps with mixture, put in baking dish and bake for 15 minutes.

Jon Bergum
Park Sparklers 4-H

Venison Italiana

Serves: 2-4
Prep Time: 1 hour

> **2 lbs. venison tenderloin**
> **flour**
> **salt and pepper**
> **1 15½ oz. jar spaghetti sauce**
> **8 oz. mozzarella cheese, shredded**

Slice partially frozen venison tenderloin into ¼-inch pieces. Pat dry with paper towel. Dredge in flour, salt and pepper. Brown meat in hot oil. Place half of the meat in a greased baking dish. Pour half of the spaghetti sauce over the meat and top with half the mozzarella cheese. Repeat so that you have 2 layers of meat, sauce and cheese. Bake, uncovered, at 350 degrees for 35 minutes.

Daniel Weber
Ham Lakers 4-H

Venison Fruit Stew

Serves: 4-6
Prep Time: 1 hour

1½ **lbs. venison steak, cubed**
  1 **T. oil**
  1 **T. vinegar**
  1 **bay leaf**
  ½ **cup onion, chopped**
  ¼ **cup raisins**
  6 **prunes**
  4 **dried apricots**
  1 **baking apple, sliced**
    salt
  ⅛ **tsp. ginger**
  2 **T. flour**

Place oil in the frying pan and brown the steak cubes. Add
1½ cups water, bay leaf, ginger, vinegar, onion and dried
fruit. Simmer for ½ hour. Add apple and simmer for 15
minutes. Make a thickening with ½ cup water and 2 T. flour.
Add thickening to the mixture until gravy texture is reached.
Serve over mashed potatoes.

George Haberman
Anoka County 4-H

Venison Chili

Serves: 6-8
Prep Time: 1 hour

- 2 lbs. ground venison
- 1 lb. ground beef
- ½ green pepper, chopped
- 3 stems celery, sliced
- 2 med. onions, chopped
- 3 lg. cloves garlic, chopped
- 2 T. chili powder
- 2 T. jalapeno peppers
- 1 can kidney beans
- 1 qt. tomatoes, chopped
- 1 lg. can tomato paste
- 1 lg. can tomato sauce
- 4-5 shakes Tabasco

Brown meat and vegetables with chili powder. Add tomato paste, mix well. Add tomatoes and sauce. Add beans and stir well. Simmer, covered, for 45 minutes.

Bonnie Dircks
Anoka County 4-H

Pheasant Wild Rice Hotdish

Serves: 4-6
Prep Time: 1 hour

 1 **pheasant, cooked and deboned**
 4 **cups wild rice, cooked**
 ¼ **cup butter**
 1 **med. onion, chopped**
4-8 **oz. fresh mushrooms, sliced**
 3 **stems celery, sliced**
 1 **T. Lawrey's Seasoned Salt**
 1 **can cream of mushroom soup**
 ⅓ **cup milk**

Saute vegetables while cooking rice and pheasant. Drain and debone pheasant, cut into bite-size pieces. Mix vegetables, rice, pheasant, soup thinned with milk, and seasoned salt in casserole dish. Cover and bake at 325 degrees for 45 minutes or microwave on medium for 15 minutes.

Bonnie Dircks
Anoka County 4-H

Duck with Orange Gravy

Serves: 2-4
Prep Time: 1 hour

  1 **mallard**
1-2 **T. Crisco**
  1 **orange, peeled and sectioned**
    celery sticks
5-6 **carrots, peeled**
    orange juice

Heat 4-quart pressure cooker on medium heat, melt Crisco. Wash duck and pat dry with paper towel. Salt and pepper bird and brown on all sides in oil. Remove bird from cooker and fill cavity with 1 orange slice up front, carrot sticks and celery sticks and 1 more orange slice. Place bird on meat rack in cooker and place more orange slices on top of bird. Add about 1½ cups of carrot pieces around bird and fill cooker ¼ to ⅓ full with orange juice. Clean rim of cooker before covering. Cook under pressure approximately ½ hour and cool cooker immediately under water. Remove bird and carrots onto platter, covering with tin foil. Discard orange slices and celery sticks. Thicken orange juice with cornstarch. Serve with rice.

Holly Herman
Rocky Raccoon 4-H

Woodcock in Chablis

Serves: 4-6
Prep Time: 6 hours

6-8 woodcock
2 onions, sliced
1 cup fresh mushrooms, sliced
1 stick butter
¼ cup Chablis
flour

Remove breasts from bones. Place in shallow dish. Cover with water and cook for 3 to 6 hours. Saute onions, add mushrooms and continue to saute. Remove onions and mushrooms, add butter and heat. Remove woodcock from water, pat dry. Save liquid. Place woodcock in butter. When edges of meat turn white, turn, add sauteed onions, mushrooms and wine. Make gravy base from red liquid by adding flour. Pour gravy onto woodcock, serve on toast for breakfast.

Andrew Stevens
Loganberries 4-H

Squirrel Jambalaya

Serves: 4
Prep Time: 2 hours

       4 squirrels
         salt and pepper
       2 lg. onions
       2 stalks celery
       1 clove garlic
      ⅛ green pepper
       4 T. parsley
       1 cup uncooked rice
  1½ cups water

Cut squirrel into pieces. Add water, cook with vegetables and spices. Remove meat from bones, discard bones. Add rice to meat and broth. Cook 20 to 30 minutes or until rice is done.

Andrew Stevens
Loganberries 4-H

Father & son recipes

Bob and Matt Allen

Take Your Boy Hunting, And You'll Never Have To Hunt For Him

by Bob Allen
President, Bob Allen Companies, Inc.

Most boys learn about guns, shooting and hunting from their dads. In my case, my dad was born in Ireland where guns and hunting are not available to the average person. He had no knowledge of them, whatsoever, and actually had some fear of guns.

Although my mother was an Iowa farm girl, and came from a family that had been involved in hunting and shooting, she went along with my dad's feelings, and as a consequence, when as a young boy, I wanted to have a BB gun, my parents elected to not allow me to have one until I was 12 years old.

At that point, most of my peers were graduating to .22 rifles or shotguns, and I found myself ashamed to go out in the woods with my gun. This led me to buying a single-shot .22 without my parents knowledge and hiding it in a hollow tree in the woods near home so that I could start out from the house with a BB gun, pick up the rifle, and actually do my hunting with the .22, replacing it in the hollow tree on my way home. My parents, in their ignorance when it came to guns, assumed that some of the squirrels and rabbits I shot had been killed with the BB gun.

To this day, I have a strong hunch that their reticence in allowing me to have guns may have intensified my desire for them; it often seems to work this way. If parents try to keep something from their children, then the children want it all the more.

On the other side of the coin, I had a friend whose burning desire was to have a son and make a hunter out of him. From the time the boy could walk, the dad dragged him along on various outings and tried in every possible way to include the son in his outdoor plans. It didn't take, and soon the boy balked at even going out with his father, much to his dad's disappointment. As it later turned out, the boy's interests were in other things, and once his dad realized this and stopped pushing, they developed a good father/son relationship.

When my son Matt was born, naturally I had hopes that he would share my love of the outdoors. The knowledge of my friend's experience with his son, and the recollection of my own boyhood, led me to use some psychology of my own to assure that Matt would enjoy hunting with me.

I started by taking him out to the gun club with me, and I did this just part of the time. I tied it in with some weekend camping expeditions. About this state in his life, Matt was going through a period in which he was fascinated by knives, hatchets and matches. He had innocently hacked up some good trees at home already, and I was fearful what the fascination with matches might lead to, so I planned some outings where he could get it all out of his system.

On these outings, we would go first to the local gun club where Matt would accompany me to the trap or skeet field. The we would head for a timbered area in a riverbottom nearby. I would get out the hatchet and knife and let Matt vent his energy for a while in gathering firewood. Then I'd let him build the fire and we would cook hotdogs or small steaks and sit around talking about the wonders of the outdoors, hunting, etc.

We did this even in cold snowy weather, and both of us looked forward to these outings. They presented a great showcase to use in introducing Matt to all the aspects of the great outdoors. The result was just what I wanted—to whet Matt's appetite for these outdoor activities.

As he grew older, I bought him a BB gun and taught him gun safety, and also, began to teach him instinct shooting in our backyard. By the age of seven or eight, he got so he could hit small objects thrown in the air, and this became the trick-shooting act which we still perform together.

I let Matt accompany me, along with some of my friends, on a few pheasant hunts. He would carry his BB gun and work the fields with us. I told him that when I could hunt all day with him and not find myself looking down the barrel muzzle of his gun or see him do anything unsafe, then I would consider getting him a real gun.

When he was about nine years old, I bought a 28 gauge shotgun for him and had it cut down so that it just about fit him. I told him that when it did fit him properly, so that he could hold it comfortably, I would start him shooting skeet, and, possibly, hunting.

Practically every week, Matt would get the gun out of the gun cabinet and, with me watching, try to see if it fit properly. All of the time I was constantly stressing the great responsibility of handling real guns and building in him a second nature for the awareness of safety.

It wasn't too long before the 28 gauge fit him, and Matt started skeet shooting with me. After a spring and a summer of skeet, I invited him on his first hunt that fall. I was really pleased at his attitude on gun handling. He even ended up being critical of some of the gun handling habits demonstrated by my friends, and, in a few instances, justifiably so.

At age 13, Matt and I went on an African safari and hunted in Mozambique together. This turned out to be the greatest experience of both our lives, and we really came to know and respect each other. Because we were hunting dangerous game such as cape buffalo, I began treating Matt as an adult, and it really paid off. I felt that if I could turn a 13 year old boy loose in Africa with a white hunter and trackers to hunt one of the most dangerous animals in the world, he most certainly deserved treatment as a grown-up. This really matured Matt, and from then on I allowed him to hunt by himself and with his friends. He always demonstrated good hunting and gun handling habits.

We've had many wonderful hunts together, and we hunt every fall. Matt has developed into a fine game shot and now shares my love of hunting—not necessarily for the shooting or the actual killing of birds and animals, but for the wonderful camaraderie, the camp life, and the exciting and beautiful world of the outdoors.

The camaraderie of a father/son hunting team just cannot be improved upon. There are few things that a father and his son can do together that weld relationships like hunting does. I've heard the late Herb Parsons, Winchester's famous exhibition shooter, say it many times, "Take your boy hunting, and you'll never have to hunt for your boy!"

Pheasant Divan

Serves: 4
Prep Time: 1 1/2 hours

  3-4 **pheasants, mainly breasts, cooked & deboned**
    2 **10 oz. packages frozen broccoli spears**
    2 **cans cream of chicken soup**
    1 **cup real Mayonnaise**
    1 **tsp. lemon juice**
    1 **cup shredded cheddar cheese**
   ¾ **cup dry bread crumbs**
    1 **stick butter**

Mix together the soup, mayo and lemon juice. Cook broccoli. Drain and arrange in an 8x12 baking dish. Place pheasant pieces on top of broccoli. Pour soup mixture on top of this & then sprinkle shredded cheese over all.
Mix stick of butter with 3/4 cups bread crumbs in skillet—sprinkle on top of casserole. Bake at 350 degrees for one hour.

Three generations of the Buck family are active in managing the knifemaking company today. Left, Chuck Buck, Al Buck and Chuck Buck, Jr.

"The Hunting Family" Has Special Meaning To The Bucks

by Charles T. "Chuck" Buck
President, Buck Knives Inc.

When we talk about family at "Buck" Knives, the word carries a lot of special meaning for us. Every one of the good people who work with us are a part of the Buck Family, in a very real sense.

But to me, family is a very personal matter, too. I learned how to make knives from my dad, Al, who is chairman of the board. He learned his knifemaking skills from his father, H.H. Buck. It was Grandpa, of course, who started it all back at the turn of the century. He thought we could make a *better* knife...and he did! We work hard at accomplishing that same goal today.

My son, Chuck Jr., is a key part of our management team now, and we're waiting for his two-year-old on, Josh, to grow up just a little more so we can pass on the knifemaking skills to our fifth generation.

The outdoors is a big part of our lives, too. One of our favorite projects is the "Buck Grand Slam." Our goal is to bag one North American Buck each year.

My son and I take part in these annual hunts, accompanied by four outdoor writers and professional guides. New Buck products are used by all participants, so it provides a great field test and instant feedback.

In November, 1984 we went to Saratoga, Wyoming in search of pronghorn antelope. Both of us scored, and Chuck Jr. had the better trophy of the two.

Mule deer were the target in November, 1985 in Montana. Again we both scored, and Chuck Jr. had the best trophy of the hunt.

Last year, I must confess, we were both blanked in our quest for blacktail on Queen Charlotte Islands in Canada, but the family honor was upheld by my son-in-law Joe Houser, who was on his first hunt.

Family togetherness—in the outdoors, in our business lives and in our commitment to God—is the Buck keystone.

Venison Pot Roast

Serves: 4
Prep Time: 6 1/2 hours

2 lbs. venison roast
2 medium potatoes, cut in pieces
1 medium onion, chopped
1 12 oz. can stewed tomatoes
1 15 oz. can tomato sauce
2 carrots, cut in pieces
1 celery stalk, cut in pieces
2 garlic cloves, minced
½ cup flour
2 T. vegetable oil
½ tsp. salt
½ tsp. pepper

Rinse roast and roll in mix of flour, salt and pepper. Place roast in dutch oven with oil at medium heat. Turn to brown on all sides. Add all vegetables, minced garlic and tomatoes. Cover pot and cook at low heat for six hours. Blend remaining juices and vegetables to create a very tasty gravy.

Roy Weatherby

The Weatherby's
Created Memories

by Ed Weatherby
President, Weatherby Firearms

It's dark. The door creaks. The dishes rattle. Who's up? Who's in the kitchen? Suddenly, I hear the familiar call. It's dad! Immediately I spring from my bed, remembering today's the long awaited day. I need to hurry. I gather my boots, my jacket, my knife. And, oh yes, my gun. It's opening day. As if it were only yesterday, I remember.

Now, I'm the one in the kitchen and my son rushes down to hurry me along. He's anxious for today. It's his first hunt.

Only now do I realize that the fun and enjoyment I had as a child on hunts with my father cannot compare with what he was experiencing. To share the excitement, to participate in the communication, to build an intimate relationship with one's child while afield, is indeed rewarding.

I remember a story about an old man who was questioned by his grandson, "After all the years you've lived, what is the most important thing you have done?" The grandfather replied, "Creating memories. For, son, I can't remember the day I moved a pile of papers from one side of my desk to the other, but I sure do remember in detail all the hunting and fishing trips I took with your father."

I'm sure my father can remember in detail the first hunt he and I made together. I respect and appreciate the fact that he felt this was important enough for him to spend his valuable time with me. Looking back in retrospect, I see how easy it would have been for him to have postponed or cancelled that day because he was so busy in his work.

Now, as a father of four children, I am keenly aware of the opportunity I have before me to develop the interest of hunting and shooting in my children. Living in the city as we do makes it more difficult, but already they're practicing in the backyard with pellet guns. It is developoing their marksmanship and safe firearms handling skills. They all look forward, as do I, to those days we will spend afield. It will take a conscious effort on my part to assure we go on those hunts. I have made a commitment to make this a priority for I believe there is a lot of validity in the saying, "If you take time to hunt with your son, you won't have to hunt for him."

Ed Weatherby

Elk, Venison or Moose Oven Burgundy

Serves: 6-8
Prep Time: 3½ hours

- 2 **T. soy sauce**
- 2 **T. flour**
- 2 **pounds venison, elk or moose stew meat**
- 4 **carrots**
- 2 **large onions**
- 1 **cup celery, thinly sliced**
- 1 **garlic clove, minced**
- ¼ **tsp. pepper**
- ¼ **tsp. marjoram**
- ¼ **tsp. thyme**
- 1 **cup burgundy, or any dry red wine**
- 1 **cup mushrooms, sliced**

Blend soy sauce with flour in a 3-quart baking dish. Cut meat into 1½-inch cubes. Add meat to soy sauce mixture and toss to coat the meat cubes.

Cut carrots into chunks, slice onions and celery, add minced garlic along with the pepper, marjoram, thyme and wine to the meat. Stir gently to mix. Cover tightly and oven simmer at 325 degrees for 2 hours.

Add mushrooms and again stir gently. Cover tightly and bake 1 hour longer or until meat and vegetables are tender. Serve with fluffy hot wild rice, noodles or mashed potatoes.

Roy and Ed Weatherby
South Gate, California

A Cry In The Swamp

by
Gerald Hunter

How often the Great American Hunter has gone afield, careful to exercise good judgment, smug to know that his vast experience has equipped him to deal with any mishap which befalls the nimrod. And then, one improbable day, a fate that's been stalking our smug lives springs upon us with a terror that dries the mouth and tears at our insides like rusty barbed wire.

I know.

It came to me on a November afternoon when I took my 10-year-old son Gerald to Georgia's Altamaha Swamp on his first real wilderness hunt. The Altamaha is a coastal river bottomland, its uninhabited part 10 to 20 miles wide and maybe 80 long, through which writhes the main river, long known for its treachery. In the swamp's ancient vastness rust the rifles of lost men who will never be found—matchlocks, blunderbusses, flintlocks, caplocks...modern autoloaders.

But perception is highly selective. We who hunt there for whitetailed deer and wild pig and turkey and duck think of our Altamaha as a lovely, if lonely, park. It gives us all year long, memories of nights around the big log fires at our hunting camp, with the adults tale-telling while the youngsters pluck ducks, where acquaintances become lifelong friends and where our growing boys learn that sportsmanship is a philosophy, not a vacation, and that in the big woods responsibility is the price of privilege. That's why, that autumn, I was introducing my son to our Middleton Lake Hunting Club of which I was president for 20 years.

The camp had gone normally, with a hunt each morning and each afternoon, and about enough game for the cookpot. I was proud of the way Gerald was learning the essentials—a boy had to learn different rules in the big woods from what he'd need for hunting around a farmstead. On the fourth day, I decided he was ready to go with me to Bug Island, a remote tract bounded on the west by the main river and cut off from our usual hunting area by a major run of the old riverbed. I loved the island, with its huge sweetgums and cypress and towering oaks and maples, because it was so utterly wild. Most hunters shunned it. I wanted Gerald to see it, feel it.

The island was too far to hike the round trip and still get much hunting done in just an afternoon. So Thursday morning after some duck shooting we packed sandwiches and told Dr. Homer Wells, our hunt director, we were heading for the island. Soon we were picking our way over rotting slabs that had once been a long logging bridge. The weather was so warm we were in shirtsleeves. I noticed some stormsign mare's tails in the blue sky but I figured we'd have another day or so of good weather.

A three-mile walk lay ahead. We took it easy so Gerald wouldn't get too tired, as I told him more about this incredible patchwork of sandy ridges choked with scrub oaks, wiregrass and frowsy grey-green palmetto. It is encircled by crazy, thickly wooded watercourses with their windfalls and moss hidden mires and innocent-looking, rotting logjams that could collapse underfoot, bounded by steep hogbacks that drop to immense virgin hardwood bottoms and cypress and gum swamps. Sometimes we followed dim logging trails, with disintegrating timber runways across the vein-work of evolved runs of the old river, runs that widened here and there to narrow, deep-woods "lakes." I could tell that Gerald wouldn't have traded this for Christmas.

I'd planned for us to just sit in a glade, on the edge of a hogback that dropped off into Homer's Hell. Homer's

Hell—named after Dr. Wells, our best woodsman, who got thoroughly lost in it—was a huge wedge of watery swampland between the island proper and the main river. But just before we reached the glade, we came across a set of fresh turkey scratchings. It looked like a big flock.

I motioned for Gerald to stop. I whispered, "Turkeys. Load your gun." Quietly he slipped a shell into the new Browning shotgun I had given him. I gestured again, and his face lit up as he put two shells into the magazine. For safety's sake, I'd never before let him load more than a single shell, so he knew this was really big business. I had loaded my own gun when we left camp.

We sat for a while, on the remote chance that the turkeys might feed back toward us. They didn't, of course. My feet got as itchy as those of a child with a new dollar.

I knew Gerald would be much too noisy to surprise a wild turkey, particularly today. I couldn't remember the woods ever being so deathly still. But the birds were just mincing along. I felt that I had a fair chance to overtake them. What a thrill Gerald would get if I could scatter the flock and he should bag one!

When I whispered my plan, Gerald nodded eagerly. I told him to sit still and watch and not to wander off, regardless, and that I wouldn't be gone very long.

As I followed the scratchings, they veered and dropped down the bluff toward Homer's Hell. That seemed odd, for turkeys usually feed uphill. Fresh hope sprang through me, for I knew a wide slough along the foot of the bluff probably would turn the birds southward. I turned for an intercept.

But I found no track along the mud-fringed slough. I thought, well, if I follow the slough northward, I'll either scatter the birds or I'll shoo 'em back toward Gerald. Soon I found where the flock had reached the water, at the remnant of a one-log runway. The birds couldn't have negotiated the half-submerged runway. They had flown across, into Homer's Hell.

My better judgment told me to give it up. But giving up isn't one of my weaknesses. I found myself doing a tight-rope act across the slick logs, and soon, finding the fresh sign. I renewed the stalk. The birds quit scratching, but I was able to follow their single file tracks to where they entered a half-acre clump of thick brush, surrounded by wet river swamp through which they couldn't escape unseen! I eased ahead, expecting them to flush momentarily.

But they stuck tight, and I couldn't find them. I'd have to wait, and hope they'd forget me.

I looked at my watch. It was 2:40 p.m. I didn't think I'd have to wait long. I had never left Gerald alone before and didn't want him to get uneasy, so I set myself a time limit of 30 minutes. I got comfortable and began watching, and started to eat my sandwiches.

No one knows better than a hunter that if you stay up quite late for several nights swapping tales around a campfire, arise before dawn, then take a good hike followed by some sandwiches and some sitting, you'll get drowsy even when you think you're alert. I haven't the faintest idea when I quit munching on my sandwich.

I was harshly awakened by the crashing of a dead limb, right beside me, to find a stiff west wind torturing the trees and a gloom so dark it looked almost like moonlight. Incessant thunder rumbled overhead and flickers of greenish lightning, with a thin, spitting crackle, played through the swamp. The sooty sky, nearly down to the treetops, stirred with turbulence. I knew immediately what was happening—a fast moving, violent cold front had swept in. It was good tornado weather. No wonder the woods had been so still, the turkeys seeking shelter! I'd been asleep for nearly two hours, and I thought: Gerald must be terrified. I grabbed up my gun jumped to my feet.

Just then, out of the west, I heard what sounded like a gunshot, followed by what might have been a faint voice calling, "Help."

I paused, cupping my ears, holding my mouth open, to hear better. But there was only the spitting thunder and the immense, heavy sound of the wind. I turned and broke into a run.

And then, in a brief respite, came three more gunshots. And this time, unmistakably, a man's voice, pitiful and wind muted, crying, "Help! Help!"

A hard chill ran through me. In the space of 10 seconds, somewhere back in my brain, the deepest elements of responsibility locked in mortal combat.

There wasn't time to hold any conference, to ponder, to weigh a trial balance. Mine was a simple choice, blunt and imminent. I could simply ignore the caller and get back to my little boy; or I could respond—and almost surely never find the slough crossing back to Gerald. Probably the man had shot himself. We'd never relocate him, if I didn't go now.

I found myself thinking back to how happy we were when Gerald was born, for he had come to us relatively late in our marriage. I remembered how we had nearly lost him, when he was four, to electrocution, and how cautious my wife always had been for his safety. She hadn't wanted me to bring him to the swamp. Her last words had been, "And don't let him out of your sight." I don't remember what I prayed, but something inside me must have cried out as desperately as the distressed stranger had done.

Thinking of what my decision might do to my little boy, I was sick inside as I dropped my gun and nonessentials beside a log, checked my compass, and hurried westward into the mucky swamp. There was never, I knew, any real choice.

The gunshots sounded as if they had come from due west. I followed by compass straight into the hard wind, watching for falling limbs and the shakiness of quagmires. With every step I sank to my boot tops. The lightning increased and thunder snapped about the opaque sky like the popping of a short-circuited, high voltage wire. There would be torrential rain any minute.

Soon I heard the gun again, louder now, and again the urgent calling. I thought: Dear God, why did there have to be a west wind; without it I'd never have heard any gunshot.

The mud deepened, and I was wallowing from tupelo root to log to brier clump. Then, all at once, I came to a willow screen. Beyond boiled the river. The water was too deep to go further, so I climbed a tree for better vision. The river was narrow here, and rising swiftly from upstream rains. I shouted, "Hello!"

My answer came immediately, from behind willows on the other bank.

The man wasn't injured. He had hunted in from somewhere in Wayne County and had been lost since early morning. He was panic-stricken and could hardly talk. I couldn't understand his name but I made out that he was from Atlanta.

I couldn't reach him, across the swift river, but I yelled that I'd get word to Jesup, and send a boat for him. I told him to stay right at the riverbank and to improvise a shelter and get some dry firewood together in a hurry. The first flailing drops of rain hit as I got down from my willow, and a grey darkness descended.

There wasn't any backtrack to follow, so I got a bearing from my compass. But in the poorer light back from the open river, I could hardly see the needle. I floundered ahead.

Behind me, then, I heard a motorboat, throttled back, cautious, a rescue boat. I turned and tried to run toward the river, shouting as I ran. I heard the motor suddenly idle down. In a moment I heard it turning up again, and the boat heading upstream with the lost man. There wasn't any way I could reach it, no way I could signal.

A wall of rain came, ice water mixed with hailstones. The temperature dropped from 65 degrees to 40. I was lost, a muddy speck in a freezing hell.

In a brief slackening of the downpour I found a slender pole, and got a good reading from my compass. I felled the pole and began dragging it behind me, its length binding against tree trunks when I tended to veer, forcing me on a more or less straight course. I became a slogging automaton, conscious of little outside my tortured mind. My thoughts were clear enough.

I wondered if Gerald had gone into hysteria, as mature hunters have done with far less provocation. Or if a limb had caught him, or if he had tried to run toward camp and broken a leg or drowned, or if he had let his gun slip.

Cold and wet as I was, my mouth was dry as tanned leather. My tongue and cheeks welded to my teeth, but I didn't care about that. There was a colder ice in my stomach, and I knew I was sobbing. Once or twice I imagined I heard, again, the far-off gunshots.

I'll never know how I came out where I did. I know that one minute I was trudging along, and the next I'd tumbled into deep water. It felt like a hot bath. If I hadn't had the pole I might have drowned. I churned around and regained the shore.

I realized that it had nearly quit raining, and that the wind had gone; and that the sky had lightened. In this pale light I began following the edge of the water, and very shortly I came to the one-log runway across the slough! The world twisted around and dropped back in place.

I began calling, running up the bluff toward where I'd left my boy.

Halfway up the bluff, Dr. Wells met me. He had on a black slicker.

"Gerald's all right," were his first words. "Scotty has just taken him back to camp." I felt my knees buckle.

Gerald had stayed put, just as I had always told him. Despite the storm, he hadn't panicked. He had found a big windfall, crouched under the roots, and gotten a fire going under its overhang. When Dr. Wells realized we might be in trouble, he had come looking. Then it had just been a matter of their exchanging gunshots.

Gerald suffered no serious effects. In the years since, he has become a better woodsman than I. Now he's raising two boys of his own. I just hope he never has to make a similar choice, but if he does, I'm sure it will be the right one.

Venison

Venison Chili

Serves: several
Prep Time: 2 hours

> 4 onions, chopped
> 2 cloves garlic, minced
> ½ cup oil
> 2 lbs. venison, cubed
> 2 4 oz. cans mushrooms
> 2 T. chili powder
> 1 tsp. ground coriander
> ½ tsp. ground cumin
> Tabasco
> 2 T. parsley
> 1 tsp. creole seasoning
> ½ tsp. cayenne pepper
> ½ tsp. oregano
> 1 cup beer
> ½ cup tomato paste
> 1½ tsp. salt
> 2-3 cans kidney or pinto beans

Saute onions and garlic in oil until soft. Add veniosn, mushrooms and cook until meat is brown. Stir in remaining ingredients except beans. Reduce heat, simmer 1-1½ hours to thicken and blend flavors. Add more beer if mixture becomes too dry. Drain beans, add and heat thoroughly just before serving.

Bill Davis
Mechanicsville, New York

Quick Stew

Serves: 4
Prep Time: ½ hour

1½ lbs. venison, chopped or ground
  1 onion
  1 can mixed vegetables
  1 can Ranch style beans
  1 small can sliced mushrooms
  ½ cup barbeque sauce or
  ½ cup picante sauce

Brown onion and meat, drain grease. Add canned goods
and juices. Stir in barbeque sauce. Simmer 10-15 minutes.
Serve hot over rice or just plain.

David Freeman
Plano, Texas

Chickoree Mountain Chili

Serves: 6-8
Prep Time: 2½ hours

  2 lbs. ground venison
  2 lg. onions
  4 garlic cloves
  1 15 oz. can whole tomatoes
  1 15 oz. can tomato sauce
  1 15 oz. can kidney beans
2-4 jalapenos
  1 T. salt
  5 T. chili powder
  ½ tsp. oregano
  2 T. bacon drippings
  ½ tsp. sugar
  ½ tsp. monosodium glutamate
  1 T. cumin
  1 T. vinegar
  1 16 oz. can of squash

Brown meat in bacon drippings. Slice onions lengthwise, add to meat. Cook for 10 to 15 minutes. Add remaining ingredients and simmer for 2 hours.

Nicholas Yurasek
Hollywood, California

Venison Crockpot Stew

Serves: 8
Prep Time: 9 hours

   2 lbs. venison
   ½ cup flour
   ½ cup vegetable oil
   1 quart water
   4 beef bouillon cubes
   1 10 oz. can tomato soup
   ½ cup mushrooms
   2 lg. potatoes, chunked
   1 lg. onion, quartered
   2 lg. carrots, cut up
   1 cup fresh or frozen peas
   1 cup fresh or frozen corn
      salt and pepper

Cut venison into 1-inch cubes. Dredge in flour and brown in oil. Combine all of the ingredients including venison and put into crockpot. Salt and pepper to taste. Mix thoroughly. Cook on low for 8 hours.

Marge Schultz
Bronson, Kansas

Crockpot Venison Stew

Serves: 6
Prep Time: 10 hours

1-2 lbs. venison steak
3-4 med. potatoes
   1 cup celery, diced
  ½ cup onion, diced
  ½ cup carrots, sliced
   1 8 oz. can tomato sauce
   2 cups beef bouillion
      salt, pepper
      basil, thyme, Tabasco
      margarine or butter

Trim fat and cut steaks into 1-inch cubes. Brown in shortening until all sides are seared. Peel and quarter potatoes. Combine all ingredients in a crockpot. Cook on low for 8-10 hours or until meat is tender.

Bill Abler, Jr.
Wyoming, Minnesota

Boxwood Venison Stew

Serves: 3-4
Prep Time: 2 hours

1½ lbs. venison, cubed
 ¼ cup flour
  2 T. butter
  1 med. onion, sliced
  1 T. celery, chopped
  1 cup mushrooms, whole
  1 bay leaf
 ½ tsp. salt
     pepper
  1 T. parsley, chopped
  1 cup water

Place venison pieces in a paper or plastic bag with flour. Shake to coat the meat. Heat the butter in a large skillet. Add meat and brown on all sides. When brown, add onion, parsley, mushrooms, bay leaf, salt, pepper and water. Once the liquid is boiling, stir, cover and reduce heat to a simmer. Cook for 1 to 1½ hours until meat is tender. Serve over noodles or rice.

Paul Phillips
Ore City, Texas

Mild Chili

Serves: 4-6
Prep Time: 1 hour

- 1 lb. ground bear, deer or elk
- ⅓ cup onion, diced
- ½ green pepper, chopped
- 1 10 oz. can tomato soup
- ¼ cup milk
- 1 19 oz. can kidney beans
- 1 can brown beans
- 2 T. brown sugar
- 1 tsp. salt
  dash pepper
- 2 dashes chili powder

Brown meat with onion and green pepper. Add remaining ingredients and simmer on low heat for ½ hour.

Glen Hill
Saskatchewan, Canada

All-Around Stew

Serves: 5-6
Prep Time: 3 hours

    2 lbs. cubed elk, venison or bear
    1 tsp. salt
    ½ tsp. pepper
      dash of paprika
    6 T. flour
    2 T. fat
    3 cups boiling water
    1 T. celery leaves, chopped
    1 onion, chopped
    2 whole cloves
    ½ cup celery, chopped
    1 cup potatoes, diced
    1 cup carrots, diced

Toss meat pieces in a mixture of salt, pepper, paprika and
flour. Heat fat in Dutch oven, sear meat on all sides. Add
boiling water, celery leaves, onion and whole cloves. Cover
tightly and simmer until almost tender, about 2½ hours. Add
vegetables and more water if necessary and continue
cooking for ½ hour.

Glen Hill
Saskatchewan, Canada

Italian Venison Meatloaf

Serves: 4-6
Prep Time: 1 hour

1½ lbs. ground venison
  1 cup Italian style bread crumbs
 ¾ cup onion, chopped
  1 8 oz. can tomato sauce
  1 egg, slightly beaten
1¼ tsp. salt
 ½ tsp. pepper
  3 hardboiled eggs
  2 T. olive oil
4-6 slices bacon (optional)

Preheat oven to 350 degrees. In a large bowl combine venison, ¾ cup bread crumbs, onion, tomato sauce, egg, salt and pepper. Mix gently but thoroughly. If desired, place bacon strips on bottom of loaf pan. Place about half of the mixture in pan. Place 3 hardboiled eggs lengthwise down the center of the meat. Pat remaining meat over eggs to form a rounded loaf. Combine remaining bread crumbs with olive oil and press evenly over loaf. Bake until cooked through, approximately 45 to 50 minutes.

Greg Kowalczyk
Blasdell, New York

Venison Meat Loaf

Serves: 2-4
Prep Time: 1¼ hours

  1 **lb. ground venison**
  ½ **lb. ground pork**
  1 **egg**
  ½ **cup dried bread crumbs**
  ½ **T. onion, chopped**
  ½ **tsp. salt**
  1 **cup milk**

Beat egg, add milk and bread crumbs. Mix thoroughly with
the meat and seasonings. Bake for 1 hour in a greased pan
at 350 degrees.

Marge Schultz
Bronson, Kansas

Venison Meatloaf

Serves: 4
Prep Time: 1½ hours

Meatloaf:
- 4 T. butter
- ¾ cup onion, chopped
- ½ cup celery, chopped
- ½ cup bell peppers, chopped
- ¼ cup scallions, chopped
- 2 tsp. garlic, minced
- 1 T. Tabasco
- 1 T. Worcestershire
- 1½ cup catsup
- 1½ lb. ground venison
- ½ lb. ground pork
- 1-2 eggs, beaten
- 1½ cup bread crumbs

Seasoning Mix:
- 2 whole bay leaves
- 1 T. salt
- 1 tsp. ground red pepper
- 1 tsp. black pepper
- ½ tsp. white pepper
- ½ tsp. ground cumin
- ½ tsp. ground nutmeg

Combine seasoning mixture in a small bowl and set aside. Melt butter in a 1-quart sauce pan over medium heat. Add onions, celery, peppers, scallions, garlic, Tabasco, Worcestershire and seasoning mix. Saute over moderate heat, stirring occasionally, scraping bottom of pan well (it should start to stick to the bottom as it cooks). Stir in catsup. Continue cooking for 2 more minutes. Remove from heat and cool. Mix ground venison, pork and eggs, cooked vegetable mixture (remove bay leaf) and bread crumbs by hand and place into loaf pan. Bake at 350 degrees for ½ hour. Top with additional catsup and bake at 400 degrees for an additional ½ hour. Cool, cut into thick slices and serve.

Bob Dubuque
Walpole, Massachusetts

Venison Ring Bologna

Serves: several
Prep Time: all day

2½ lbs. venison
2½ lbs. pork shoulder
½ cup salt
½ cup sugar
¼ tsp. sodium nitrate
1½ tsp. white pepper
⅜ tsp. nutmeg

¼ tsp. coriander
⅝ tsp. allspice
⅛ tsp. garlic powder
½ tsp. paprika
2 cups cold water
½ tsp. liquid smoke
hog casings

Prepare the hog casings by soaking in water for 1 hour. Mix all dry spices together. Stir well. Add water and liquid smoke. Grind the meat. Chill. Run the meat through the grinder a second time, using a cutting plate with ⅛-inch holes. Thoroughly mix the meat with the spice mixture. A grayish-brown color indicates complete mixing. Stuff the mixture lightly into the casings. Tie the ends together to form rings. Cook either in water or in the oven. The water temperature should be 160 to 175 degrees. Drop the rings into the water and cook until they float, about 1 to 2 hours. To cook in the oven, hang the rings from the top rack, place foil on the bottom of the oven to catch drips. Insert a meat thermometer into the center of one ring. Oven temperature should be 200 degrees. Cook meat until internal temperature reaches 160 to 175 degrees. Quickly cool meat by immersing in cold water, then refrigerate.

Carole Lent
Limestone, New York

Venison Sausage

Serves: several
Prep Time: 4 days

- 1 **lb. ground venison**
- 1 **rounded tsp. Morton's Tender Quick Salt**
- ½ **tsp. mustard seed**
- ½ **tsp. garlic salt**
  peppercorns

Mix the above ingredients well. Store in refrigerator in covered bowl for three days. Mix once each day. On the fourth day shape into a roll and bake at 175 degrees for 4½ hours.

Dana L. Harris
Eden Prairie, Minnesota

Special Burgers

Serves: 2-4
Prep Time: 15 minutes

- 1 lb. ground venison
- ¼ cup catsup
- 1 T. mustard
- 1 tsp. vinegar
- 1 T. Worcestershire
- 1 tsp. sugar
- ½ cup milk
   dash of salt

Mix all ingredients thoroughly. Spread on hamburger bun halves. Place under broiler for 2 to 5 minutes until done.

Mike Gaddy
Nunda, New York

High Speed Venison

Serves: 4
Prep Time: 1¼ hours

- 2-3 lbs. venison steaks
- 1 pkg. onion soup mix
- 1 can cream of mushroom soup
- 2 beef bouillon cubes
- 2 onions, sliced
- ¾ cup milk
   salt and pepper

Trim fat off steaks and brown in skillet. Mix together the mushroom soup, onion soup mix and milk. Pour over steaks. Add onions and bouillon. Simmer 1 hour. Serve over rice.

Rick Johnson
Pontiac, Michigan

Venison Bleu Cheese Burgers

Serves: 8
Prep Time: all day

   2 **lbs. ground venison**
   ½ **cup red wine**
   2 **tsp. salt**
   ¼ **tsp. pepper**
   1 **onion, grated**
   1 **clove garlic, chopped**
   ½ **cup butter**
   ½ **cup bleu cheese**
   ½ **cup red wine**
   2 **tsp. minced parsley**

Mix venison, wine, salt, pepper, onion and garlic thoroughly.
Refrigerate for several hours. Form mixture into 8 patties.
Cook burgers until done in melted butter. Crumble bleu
cheese on top of patties and cover for a few minutes before
removing from skillet. Stir wine and minced parsley into
remaining juice. Heat and serve over burgers.

Stewart Rolf
San Francisco, California

Meatballs

Serves: 4-6
Prep Time: 1¼ hours

- 1 **lb. ground venison**
- 1 **lb. ground pork shoulder**
- ½ **cup milk**
- 1 **cup soda crackers, crushed**
- 1 **egg**
- ¼ **tsp. pepper**
  salt

Sauce:
- 1½ **cups brown sugar**
- 1 **tsp. dry mustard**
- ½ **cup vinegar**
- ½ **cup water**

Mix thoroughly the ground meat, milk, crackers and egg. Add salt and pepper to taste. Shape into meatballs 2 to 3 inches in diameter and put in roasting pan. Combine sauce ingredients, pour over meatballs. Bake, covered for ½ hour in 350 degree oven. Turn meatballs and bake for an additional ½ hour. Onions can be added to this dish as it bakes.

Walter Squier
Portland, Connecticut

Barbeque Venison Meatballs

Serves: 6-8
Prep Time: 45 minutes

1 lb. ground venison	Sauce:
½ tsp. pepper	½ cup catsup
1 tsp. salt	2 T. Worcestershire
⅔ cup milk	2 tsp. vinegar
¾ cup oatmeal	2 tsp. brown sugar
2 T. oil	1 tsp. yellow mustard
chopped onion	

Combine meat, seasonings, milk and oatmeal. Shape into small meatballs. Brown in hot oil. Mix all sauce ingredients. Heat in sauce pan. Place meatballs in a casserole dish. Pour hot sauce over meatballs, cover and bake at 350 degrees for ½ hour. Serve on small plates with toothpicks.

John Zanon
Norway, Michigan

Poontock

Serves: 3-4
Prep Time: 1 hour

2-3 lbs. venison
  1 lg. onion, chopped
  1 lg. lemon, peeled and sliced

Salt, pepper and flour venison, fry until light brown on both sides. Remove meat and place in a large pot. Add onion and lemon. Cover contents with water and cook over low heat. Allow to slow boil for 30 minutes to 1 hour. It makes its own gravy. Serve with rice or potatoes.

Bill Morrison
Camden, Arkansas

Venison Lasagna

Serves: 8
Prep Time: 1 hour

2 lbs. ground venison
1 32 oz. jar spaghetti sauce
1 lb. ricotta cheese
½ lb. mozzarella cheese
2 eggs, beaten
1 tsp. parsley flakes
  salt and pepper
1 lb. lasagna noodles, cooked
1 cup grated Parmesan cheese

Brown venison in large skillet. Add spaghetti sauce. Heat to boiling. Cut thin slices of mozarella for topping and shred the rest. Mix shredded cheese with the ricotta cheese, eggs, parsley, salt and pepper. Oil two 12x8-inch pans. Ladle a cup of sauce into the bottom of each pan. Layer with noodles, then cheese mixture. Repeat twice, top with mozzarella slices and sprinkle with Parmesan cheese. Cover with foil and bake at 350 degrees for 30 to 40 minutes.

Vernon Loggdon
Aiva, Oklahoma

Lasagna

Serves: 6
Prep Time: 1 hour

- ½ **lb. ground elk or venison**
- 1 **cup onion, chopped**
- 2 **lg. cloves garlic, minced**
- 2 **T. oregano**
- 1 **pint cottage or ricotta cheese**
- 2 **cans tomato soup**
- ½ **cup water**
- 2 **tsp. vinegar**
- ½ **lb. lasagna noodles, cooked**
- ½ **lb. mozzarella cheese, thinly sliced**
  grated Parmesan cheese

In saucepan, brown meat and cook onion, garlic, oregano. Add soup, water and vinegar. Simmer 30 minutes. In baking pan arrange three alternate layers of noodles, cheese, meat sauce, mozzarella. Top with Parmesan. Bake at 350 degrees for ½ hour. Let stand 15 minutes.

Glen Hill
Saskatchewan, Canada

Venison Jerky

Serves: several
Prep Time: 24 hours

- ¾ **cup soy sauce**
- ¾ **cup Worcestershire**
- ½ **bottle liquid smoke**
- 2 **tsp. seasoned salt**
- 2 **tsp. Accent**
- 2 **tsp. onion powder**
- ⅔ **tsp. garlic powder**
- ⅔ **tsp. black pepper**
  Tabasco

Debone and remove the fat from meat. Cut into strips about ⅛-inch thick. Mix all ingredients together. Marinate meat in mixture overnight. Lay marinated strips over oven racks with a cookie sheet underneath. Bake in oven on low temperature for 4 to 6 hours, turning over halfway through to be sure both sides are dried. Be sure to use low temperature, 125-140 degrees works best.

Bill Abler, Sr.
Wyoming, Minnesota

Ground Venison Jerky

Serves: several
Prep Time: 3-4 hours

    wax paper
  5 **lbs. ground venison**
1½ **tsp. Morton's Quick Salt**
  3 **T. salt**
  2 **tsp. black pepper**
  2 **tsp. garlic powder**
  1 **tsp. cayenne pepper**
1½ **tsp. cardamons**
  1 **tsp. marjoram**
  2 **tsp. Accent**
  1 **oz. liquid smoke**
  1 **oz. water**
  1 **oz. vinegar**

Mix ground venison with the spices. Roll between wax paper to ¼-inch thickness. Mix liquid smoke, vinegar and water, brush on meat. Bake at lowest temperature for 3 to 4 hours with oven door ajar. When meat is dry, cut into strips and store in tight container.

Warna Reed
Matherville, Illinois

Fried Venison Heart or Liver

Serves: 2
Prep Time: ½ hour

- **3 hearts or 2 livers**
  pepper
- **1 T. sugar**
- **½ stick butter**

Slice meat into 1-inch slices. Boil slices in water for 20 minutes. Drain. Place slices in pan with ½ stick butter. Mix pepper and sugar together and set aside. Fry slices approximately 5 to 10 minutes. Sprinkle sugar mixture over slices while frying.

Dwylan Reigel
Lebanon, Pennsylvania

Catskill Venison Liver Pate

Serves: several
Prep Time: 1 hour

1 **deer liver**
1 **bay leaf**
1 **onion, sliced**
6 **eggs**
4 **onions**
6 **saltine crackers**
½ **cup mayonnaise**
3 **T. horseradish**
2 **T. Worcestershire**
2 **tsp. garlic powder**
 Tabasco to taste

Boil liver with bay leaf and sliced onion until cooked, about 30 minutes. Boil eggs and peel onions. Slice the boiled liver, eggs and onions. Mix. Put mixture through a grinder and add saltine crackers through last. Blend in remaining ingredients. Serve on crackers.

Hank Starr
Monticello, New York

Chinese Venison with Vegetables

Serves: 4-6
Prep Time: 1 hour

  1 **lb. venison, cut into strips**
  2 **T. oil**
  ½ **lb. fresh mushrooms, sliced**
  1 **onion, sliced and separated into rings**
  1 **green pepper, sliced**
  ½ **cup celery, sliced**
  1 **clove garlic, minced**
  ½ **cup water**
  3 **T. soy sauce**
  1 **6 oz. pkg. frozen pea pods**
  1 **pint cherry tomatoes**
  2 **T. cornstarch**
  2 **T. water**
    hot cooked rice

Cut and assemble all ingredients. Heat wok. Add oil and heat. Add venison, cook and stir until meat loses its pink color, about 5 minutes. Add onion, pepper, garlic and celery, cook and stir 3 minutes. Add mushrooms, cook and stir 1 minute. Mix ½ cup water and soy sauce, add to wok, cover and reduce heat. Cook 3 minutes. Add pea pods and tomatoes, cover and continue cooking for 3 minutes. Dissolve cornstarch in 2 T. water, stir into meat mixture. Cook and stir until mixture bubbles and thickens. Serve over hot rice.

Jack Hornung
Cheektowaga, New York

Sweet and Sour Venison

Serves: 4
Prep Time: 1 hour

- **2 lbs. cubed venison**
- **2 T. oil**
- **¼ cup water**
- **1 15 oz. can pineapple chunks**
- **⅓ cup packed brown sugar**
- **2 T. cornstarch**
- **¼ tsp. ground ginger**
- **¼ cup cider vinegar**
- **2½ T. soy sauce**
- **salt**
- **hot cooked rice**

In a large skillet, brown the venison in oil. Add the water, cover and simmer for 25 minutes. Meanwhile, drain the pineapple, reserving the juice. Combine the sugar, cornstarch, ginger and salt. Blend in reserved pineapple juice, vinegar and soy sauce. Add to the venison. Cook and stir until thickened. Stir in pineapple chunks and heat through. Serve over rice.

Judie Weseman
Idleyld Park, Oregon

Venison Chow Mein

Serves: 8-10
Prep Time: 1 hour

- **2 lbs. cubed venison**
- **2 lg. onions, sliced**
- **1 stalk celery, sliced**
- **½ lb. bean sprouts**
- **1 sm. can bamboo shoots**
- **1 sm. can mushrooms, chopped**
- **soy sauce**
- **salt and pepper**

Brown venison in large skillet, then transfer to 4-quart stew pot. Cover with 10 cups water and boil for ½ hour. Add onions, celery and boil until tender. Add bean sprouts, bamboo shoots and mushrooms and boil for 10 minutes. Serve with chow mein noodles.

Dennis Sharp
Clifton, Arizona

Venison Teriyaki

Serves: 6
Prep Time: 8 hours

- 2 lbs. venison steak
- 1 cup Lite soy sauce
- 1 cup Hiram Walker Creme de Cassis
- 1 T. ground ginger
- 1 T. garlic powder
- 1 T. honey
- 1 T. cooking oil
- ½ tsp. black pepper
  juice of ½ lemon

Put the marinade ingredients in a large bowl and mix well. Cut the steak into ¼-inch thick strips. Put the steak strips into the marinade and let sit overnight. Remove the steak from the marinade and let drain for ½ hour. Place the strips on bamboo or steel skewers and cook lightly over coals. Do not overcook as they dry out fast.

Dick Derochea
Whitman, Massachusetts

Venison and Cabbage

Serves: 3
Prep Time: 3½ hours

- 1 lb. ground venison
- ⅓ cup uncooked rice
- 2 T. butter
- 1 onion, sliced thin
- 1 tsp. sugar
- 1 can tomato soup
- 6 lg. cabbage leaves
  juice of 1 lemon
- 1 egg, well beaten
- 1 tsp. minced parsley
- 1 tsp. chopped celery
  salt and pepper

Season meat well with salt and pepper, and add the egg. Mix with rice. Make a sauce by melting butter in a skillet. When brown, add the onion and cook for several minutes. Combine the tomato soup and an equal amount of water and add to the browned onion. Season with lemon juice, sugar, salt, pepper, parsley and celery. Cook 10 minutes. Wash cabbage leaves and boil until limp. Put 2 T. meat mixture in each cabbage leaf and roll tightly. Fasten each roll with a toothpick. Place rolls in a sauce pan, pour sauce over and cover tightly. Cook slowly over a low fire for 3 hours. Serve very hot with your favorite potatoes.

W.V. Hepler
Monroe, Utah

Venison Diane

Serves: 6
Prep Time: 1 hour

1½ lbs. venison steaks, ½-inch thick
  ½ tsp. coarse ground pepper
    salt
1½ tsp. dry mustard
  ¼ cup oil
  1 cup sliced mushrooms
  3 T. fresh lemon juice
  1 T. minced chives
  2 tsp. Worcestershire
  ¼ cup brandy (optional)

Pound each steak to ⅓-inch thickness. Sprinkle each side
with salt. Blend pepper and mustard, pound into both sides
of meat. In skillet heat oil to sizzling. Add half of the steaks,
saute 2 minutes on each side. Transfer to hot serving plate
and keep warm. Repeat for remaining steaks. In same pan,
saute mushrooms in drippings until tender. With slotted
spoon, place mushrooms over steaks. Add lemon juice,
chives and Worcestershire to drippings, bring to a boil. To
flame, heat brandy to lukewarm in saucepan, flame and
add to skillet. When flames subside, pour over steaks. Serve
immediately.

Greg Kowalczyk
Blasdell, New York

Venison Taco Salad

Serves: 6
Prep Time: 1½ hour

- 6 **potatoes**
- 1 **lb. ground venison**
- 8 **oz. sour cream**
- 6 **oz. mozzarella cheese**
- 6 **taco shells**
- 1 **can chilies**
- 1 **envelope taco sauce**
- 1 **can tomato paste**
- 2 **tomatoes**
- ¼ **head lettuce**

Bake potatoes. Brown venison, add sauce, chilies, tomato paste. Mix cheese and sour cream together. Cut potatoes into quarters, pour cheese and sour cream over top. Bake at 350 degrees until cheese melts. After cheese is melted, put meat mixture over top. Dice lettuce and tomatoes, crush taco shells into large pieces. Place on top of meat.

Dwylan Reigel
Lebanon, Pennsylvania

Venison Stroganoff

Serves: 4
Prep Time: 1½-2 hours

1 **lb. venison, cut into strips**
1 **lg. onion, chopped**
2 **T. margarine**
1 **cup sour cream**
1 **can beef consomme**
1 **can mushroom slices**
2 **T. flour**
1 **8 oz. can tomato sauce**
1 **tsp. soy sauce**
   salt and pepper

Saute onion in margarine. Add meat and salt and pepper to taste. Brown meat. Take from heat and stir in flour, tomato sauce and mushrooms. Add sour cream and consomme alternately. Add soy sauce, return to heat and simmer for 1½ hours or until meat is tender. Serve over rice or noodles.

Robert Farland
Ellsworth AFB, South Dakota

Venison Stroganoff

Serves: 4
Prep Time: 1½ hours

  2 lbs. venison
  ½ tsp. salt
  ¼ tsp. pepper
  1 stick butter
  4 med. onions, sliced
  1 can beef broth
  1 4 oz. can mushrooms, drained
  5 T. flour
  1 tsp. mustard
  ⅓ cup sour cream
  ⅓ cup dry white wine

Melt butter. Brown venison, salt, pepper and onions. Add beef broth, flour and mustard. Stir well. Add mushrooms, cook 1 hour, simmer until thick. Five minutes before done, add sour cream and wine. Serve over potatoes or egg noodles.

Mrs. Herman Luedtke, Jr.
Kenosha, Wisconsin

Tender Venison

Serves: 4
Prep Time: 8 hours

1¾ lb. venison roast
1 lg. tart apple, cored and sliced
1 27 oz. can sauerkraut, drained
1 16 oz. can tomatoes, chopped and drained
¼ cup firmly packed brown sugar

Arrange apple slices in bottom of slow cooker. Place roast over apples. Add sauerkraut, tomatoes and brown sugar. Cover and cook about 8 hours on low.

Warna Reed
Matherville, Illinois

Saskatchewan Sloppy Joes

Serves: 4
Prep Time: ½ hour

¾ cup onion, chopped
1 green pepper, chopped
1 clove garlic, minced
2 T. oil
1 lb. ground venison
1 can tomatoes
1 tsp. oregano
1 tsp. parsley flakes
½ tsp. salt and pepper

In large skillet saute onion, green pepper and garlic in oil until tender. Add meat and cook until browned, stirring occasionally to break up pieces. Drain off fat, stir in remaining ingredients. Simmer, uncovered for 10 to 15 minutes. Serve over bread or on buns.

Glen Hill
Saskatchewan, Canada

Venison Burgundy

Serves: 4-6
Prep Time: 5 hours

>   2 lbs. venison stew meat, trimmed
>   1 pkg. dry onion soup mix
>   1 can golden mushroom soup
>   1 8 oz. can mushroom pieces, drained
>   ½ cup brown sugar
>   1 cup burgundy

Mix all ingredients together (do not brown meat). Place in shallow roasting pan, cover tightly with foil and bake in 250 degree oven for 5 hours. Serve over rice or noodles.

Robert Hilten
Orland Park, Illinois

Spaghetti Squash with Venison

Serves: 6-8
Prep Time: 1¼ hours

>   1 lg. spaghetti squash
>   2 lbs. ground venison
>   4 lg. onions
>   1 quart jar spaghetti sauce
>   pepper to taste
>   4 T. soy sauce

Cook squash 45 minutes at 375 degrees. Fork the squash out of its skin. Fry onions and venison in a little oil until brown. Mix everything together, let cook for 15 minutes.

Charles Riegel
Hudson, New York

Hunter's Venison

Serves: several
Prep Time: 2½ hours

3 lbs. venison
2 T. oil
1 onion, minced
1 square inch of ham, minced
1 T. flour
1 clove garlic, minced
2 sprigs thyme
2 bay leaves
½ lb. mushrooms, sliced
   juice of 1 lemon
½ bottle white wine
   salt and pepper

Cut the venison into pieces 2-inches square. Salt and pepper well. Brown venison in 2 T. oil. When nearly brown, add onion, chopped fine, and brown slightly. Add the ham, minced very fine, and the garlic, bay leaves and thyme. Add 1 T. flour and brown for a few minutes more. Add ½ bottle of white wine and let simmer for 5 minutes. Then add a quart of consomme or water and let cook for about 1 hour. Add mushrooms. Cook ½ hour longer.

Dirk Ault
Pittsburgh, Pennsylvania

Dutch Oven Venison Pot Roast

Serves: 4-6
Prep Time: 3 hours

2-3 lb. venison rump roast
2 onions, quartered
water
⅓ cup sherry
2 cloves garlic, minced
¼ tsp. each dry mustard, marjoram, rosemary, thyme, sweet basil
1 bay leaf
4 potatoes, quartered
4 carrots, sliced lengthwise
flour
salt and pepper
1 lb. mushrooms
2 T. bacon drippings
butter

Trim off all fat. Season 2 T. flour with salt and pepper to taste. Dredge roast in flour. In Dutch oven, brown roast on all sides in hot bacon drippings. Season generously with salt and pepper. Add onions, sherry, garlic, spices, bay leaf and carrots. Add water to cover. Cook at 350 degrees for 2 hours, stirring every ½ hour. Add potatoes, cook 1 additional hour or until roast and potatoes are tender. During last 10 minutes of cooking, clean, slice and saute mushrooms in butter. Remove roast and vegetables to warm platter. Remove bay leaf. Pour remaining pot juices into 4-cup bowl. Add enough water to make 3 cups of liquid. Mix 5 T. flour in small jar of water to add to pot liquid. Bring to boil in Dutch oven and cook 3 minutes. Cover sliced roast with mushrooms. Serve with gravy and beer bread.

Robert Parker
Las Vegas, Nevada

Marinated Venison Roast

Serves: 6-8
Prep Time: 8 hours

4-5 lb. venison roast
1 12 oz. can Mellow Yellow soda
⅓ cup soy sauce
⅛ tsp. garlic powder
1 lg. onion, sliced
   salt and pepper
6 T. flour

In large bowl combine first 5 marinade ingredients. Let the roast marinate for 2 hours. Turn and marinate for 2 more hours. Put the roast and marinade in a large roaster. Bake in a slow oven, 325 degrees, for 4 hours. You may have to add 1 cup water to the roaster. Thicken the marinade with the flour for gravy.

Larry Hallman
Monmouth, Illinois

Marinated Deer Steaks

Serves: 4-5
Prep Time: all day

> **3 lbs. deer steaks**
> **½ cup soy sauce**
> **½ cup red wine**
> **Goya Adobo All-Purpose Seasoning**

Cut meat into ½-inch thick strips. Sprinkle both sides of each strip with Goya Adobo. Place in bowl, cover. Allow to stand for 1 hour to soak in the seasoning. Add soy sauce and red wine, stir the meat strips until thoroughly moistened by the liquid. Do not drain. Cover the bowl and place in refrigerator until supper time. Barbeque the meat strips for a few minutes on each side. Do not over cook.

Danilo Salcedo
Youngstown, Ohio

Strip Steak Filipino

Serves: 2-4
Prep Time: 1 hour

> **1 lb. game meat, sliced thinly**
> **¼ cup stir fry sauce**
> **1 med. onion**
> **3 cloves garlic, crushed**
> **1 lg. lemon**
> **¼ cup cooking oil**

Wash meat and marinate in stir fry sauce, squeeze lemon and add juice to the rest of the ingredients except the oil. Take meat out of the sauce and fry until done. Add the remaining sauce when meat is done. Simmer and cook until sauce thickens and meat is tender.

Andy Sturgeon
Sumas, Washington

Beer Batter Venison

Serves: 4-6
Prep Time: 1 hour

- **2 lbs. venison steaks**
- **2 eggs**
- **3 cups flour**
  salt
  pepper
- **1 can beer**
  shortening

Cut steaks fairly thinly, salt and pepper both sides heavily. Beat each side with meat hammer. Beat eggs, 2 tsp. salt and 3 tsp. pepper, add to flour. Mix thoroughly. Add beer to flour mixture until batter is soupy. Dip steaks in batter. Fry on low heat until golden brown.

Don Edwards
Omaha, Texas

Potato Chip Venison

Serves: 4-6
Prep Time: 1½ hours

2-3 lbs. venison
2 tsp. tenderizer
2 tsp. Louisiana Hot Sauce
4 T. mustard
1 tsp. Worcestershire
⅔ cup vinegar

Cut venison across the grain into ¼-inch thick potato chip size slices. (Boned-out muscle or backstrap is the best.) Marinade in the above ingredients for 30 minutes (overnight in the refrigerator is better). Coat in flour just before frying. Deep fry in hot oil until golden brown, approximately 2-5 minutes. Do not overcook.

Henry Hutson
Mangham, Louisiana

Venison Shish-ka-bobs

Serves: several
Prep Time: varies

  1 **whole rump or shoulder**
  ½ **lbs. mushrooms**
  2 **baskets cherry tomatoes**
  ½ **1 lb. small white onions**
     Marinade:
  1 **T. meat tenderizer**
  1 **tsp. garlic powder**
  1 **tsp. onion powder**
  2 **cups water**
  1 **tsp. poultry seasoning**
  1 **tsp. soy sauce**
  2 **tsp. A-1 sauce**

Marinate venison cubes overnight, turning or stirring several
times. Drain well and place on skewers, alternating with
vegetables. Salt and pepper to taste. Can be baked at 375
degrees for 35-40 minutes or cooked over grill.

Denise Washburn
McKinleyville, California

Venison Delight

Serves: 6-8
Prep Time: 1-1½ hours

2-3 lbs. venison
salt
pepper
20 oz. can mushroom soup
½ lb. butter

Preheat oven to 350 degrees. Slice venison into ½-inch steaks. Tenderize, salt and pepper. Brown steaks on both sides in cast iron skillet. Melt ¼ lb. butter on cookie sheet. Arrange steaks on cookie sheet and top with remaining butter. Bake for 15 minutes. Turn steaks and bake for an additional 10 minutes. Pour off liquid. Add mushroom soup and bake for 12-15 minutes.

Richard Walls
Williams, Indiana

Jimbeaux's Venison Bambino

Serves: 8-10
Prep Time: 30 minutes

  2 **lbs. young venison backstrap**
  ¼ **cup butter**
  2 **T. lemon juice**
  1 **onion**
  2 **cloves garlic**
    sherry cooking wine
    vermicelli
    flour
    milk
    salt and pepper

Slice venison into thin medallions and place in tall container. Add just enough sherry to cover meat. Work sherry into meat with a wooden spoon. Melt butter in skillet. Slice onion thinly. Chop garlic and onion coarsely and simmer in butter for 5 minutes. Add lemon juice, meat and sherry. Cover and simmer for 10 minutes, turning meat occasionally for even cooking. Boil pasta in water. As pasta cooks, remove meat and garlic from skillet. Put meat on warm plate in oven and make a thin gravy in the skillet using flour and milk, stirring until smooth. Add meat to gravy and simmer until pasta is done. Quickly drain and serve pasta, topping with the meat and gravy.

James Kelley
Denver, Colorado

Deer Mincemeat

Prep Time: 1½ hours

- 2 **lbs. cooked ground venison**
- 4 **lbs. chopped apples**
- 2 **lbs. raisins**
- 4 **cups brown or white sugar**
- 2 **tsp. salt**
- ¾ **lb. chopped suet or butter**
- ½ **tsp. chives**
- 1 **tsp. mace**
- ½ **tsp. nutmeg**
- 1½ **tsp. cinnamon**
   apple cider

Mix ingredients thoroughly, then add enough apple cider to cover the mixture. Fruit juices may be substituted for cider or water and ½ cup vinegar may also be used. Cook very slowly until fruits are tender, about 1 hour. Put into pies or fruit jars.

Marge Schultz
Bronson, Kansas

Moose Parmesan

Serves: 2-4
Prep Time: 1 hour

> **2 lb. moose roast or thinly sliced steaks**
> **2 15 oz. cans tomato sauce**
> **flour**
> **1 tsp. garlic salt**
> **1½ tsp. oregano**
> **salt and pepper**
> **4 oz. mozzarella cheese**
> **Parmesan cheese**

Cut roast into ¼ to ½-inch slices. Combine approximately ½ to 1 cup flour and garlic powder and dredge the meat in it. In large skillet, pour only enough cooking oil to coat bottom. Fry slices of meat, turning once. Place meat in a single layer in a baking pan. Combine the tomato sauce, oregano, salt and pepper. Pour over meat. Sprinkle with Parmesan cheese and mozzarella. Bake at 350 degrees until cheese is melted. Serve over spaghetti with extra sauce.

John Holz
Ft. Wainwright, Alaska

Moose Meatloaf

Serves: 4
Prep Time: 1¼ hours

2-3 **lbs. mooseburger**
  1 **sm. can milk**
2-3 **pieces bread, crumbled**
  1 **lg. onion**
  1 **clove garlic**
3-4 **stalks celery**
2-3 **eggs**
  1 **green pepper**
  1 **can tomato sauce**

Mix all ingredients together and put into loaf pan. Bake about 45 minutes at 350 degrees. Take out of oven, pour tomato sauce over top and bake 15 minutes more. Serve with baked or scalloped potatoes.

Steven Millhollen
Tyndall AFB, Florida

Moose Bourguignon

Serves: 2-4
Prep Time: 1 hour

     T. butter
   5 med. onions, sliced
  12 oz. mushrooms, sliced
   2 lbs. moose, cubed
     garlic, minced
   4 carrots, sliced thickly
3-4 potatoes, cubed
   1 cup celery, sliced
   1 tsp. salt
  ¼ tsp. marjoram
  ¼ tsp. thyme
     pepper
   2 T. flour
   1 can beef broth
  ½ cup red burgundy

Melt butter. Cook and stir onions and mushrooms until onions are tender. Add meat and brown on all sides. Sprinkle seasonings, herbs and flour over meat. Add broth and heat until boiling. Stir while cooking. Add wine, carrots, potatoes and celery. Simmer until vegetables are tender.

John Holz
Ft. Wainwright, Alaska

Swedish Pot Moose

Serves: 4
Prep Time: 3½ hours

3-4 lb. moose roast
1 tsp. nutmeg
1 tsp. cinnamon
½ tsp. ginger
2 tsp. salt
⅛ tsp. pepper
2 sm. onions, sliced
1 clove garlic, diced
½ cup brown sugar
½ cup red wine or vinegar
½ cup water
4 bay leaves

Brown meat, add dry ingredients, water and vinegar. Simmer for 2 to 3 hours in covered pan. Add more water if necessary. Thicken gravy with corn starch.

John Holz
Ft. Wainwright, Alaska

Moose Stroganoff

Serves: 2-4
Prep Time: ½ hour

  2 lbs. moose steak or roast
  4 T. butter
  ½ T. onion, minced
  ½ lb. mushrooms, sliced
  ½ pint sour cream
    salt
    nutmeg

Pound meat very thin and cut into near finger-shaped pieces. Melt 2 T. butter in a large heavy pan. Add onion, cook and stir until onion is tender. Add moose, cook quickly, about 5 minutes on all sides. Push to one side of pan. Saute mushrooms in remaining butter. Season with salt, pepper and nutmeg and add to moose. Add sour cream, heat and season to taste. Serve over buttered noodles.

John Holz
Ft. Wainwright, Alaska

Moose Stew

Serves: 6-8
Prep Time: 3 hours

moose meat	sugar to taste
1 T. salt	lemon juice to taste
1 T. pepper	2 bay leaves
6 med. potatoes	¼ cup oil
1 lg. onion	⅓ cup flour
3-4 med. carrots	¼ stalk celery
2 whole cloves	assorted vegetables

Roll thawed moose meat in flour, salt and pepper. Fry in hot oil to brown. Add water and cook about 2 hours. Add potatoes, onions, celery, carrots, bay leaves, cloves, salt, pepper, sugar and lemon juice. Cook for 1 hour.

Steven Millhollen
Tyndall AFB, Florida

Moose Goulash

Serves: 4-6
Prep Time: 1 hour

1-2 lbs. moose meat
    celery, chopped
    green pepper, chopped
    onion, chopped
    macaroni or spaghetti noodles
  1 16 oz. can tomato sauce
  2 cups grated cheese
    garlic

Fry moose meat with celery, onions and green peppers. Add garlic. Mix with noodles. Add tomato sauce and cook about 15 minutes more. Serve with grated cheese on top.

Steven Millhollen
Tyndall AFB, Florida

Caribou and Moose Loaf

Serves: 6-8
Prep Time: 1 ¼ hours

- 3 lbs. ground caribou
- 3 lbs. ground moose
- 3 cups bread crumbs
- 6 slices bacon
- 3 eggs
- 2 cups milk
- 1 T. salt
- ½ tsp. pepper
- 1 ½ cups catsup
- 1 tsp. garlic powder
- 1 cup onion, chopped

Put all the ingredients except bacon in a large bowl. Mix thoroughly. Put in a large loaf pan and cover the mixture with 1 cup catsup. Lay the bacon slices on top. Bake at 375 degrees for about 70 minutes.

"Alaska" Rick Sinchak
Warren, Ohio

Pocket Stew

Serves: 4
Prep Time: 20 minutes

  1 lb. elk steak
  2 med. carrots
  2 stalks celery
  1 lg. potato
  2 bell peppers
  1 med. onion
  4 mushrooms
    pinch of sage
    salt and pepper
  1 T. butter

Cube steak into 1-inch squares. Slice the carrots, celery and
mushrooms thinly. Cut the potatoes and peppers into small
pieces. Divide each ingredient into 4 equal parts. Lay out 4
18-inch pieces of foil. Place one pile of each ingredient in the
middle of each piece of foil. Add a pinch of sage, salt and
pepper and ¼ T. butter. Fold the foil tightly around the
ingredients. Place one pocket stew in each hunter's pack. To
cook, place in a good bed of coals. After 10 to 15 minutes,
turn over once. Remove after 20 minutes of cooking time.
Cooks in its own juices, no water needed. Can be cooked in
an oven at 350 degrees for about 20 minutes.

Kenneth Binam
Fruita, Colorado

Saskatchewan Elk Burgers

Serves: 4-5
Prep Time: 25 minutes

  1 **lb. ground elk**
 10 **soup crackers, crushed**
  1 **egg**
  1 **T. Worcestershire**
 ½ **tsp. salt**
     pepper
  1 **med. onion, chopped**

Mix all ingredients together. Form into patties and cook on
grill.

Glen Hill
Saskatchewan, Canada

Cabbage Patch Stew

Serves: 4-6
Prep Time: 1 hour

  1 **lb. elk burger**
  1 **can stewed tomatoes**
  1 **can red kidney beans**
  1 **can chile beans**
 ½ **cup celery, chopped**
  1 **onion**
  1 **cup green chile peppers**
 ½ **head chopped cabbage**

Brown meat with onion. Cook cabbage 20 minutes in water,
then add remaining ingredients. Cook until done. Season to
taste.

Jim Sabol
Laurel, Montana

Antelope Cabbage Casserole

Serves: 1-2
Prep Time: 1 hour

  1 **lb. antelope burger**
  3 **T. butter**
  1 **onion, chopped**
  2 **T. parsley, chopped**
  ¼ **tsp. pepper**
  ½ **tsp. basil**
  1 **medium head cabbage**
  1 **can tomato soup**

Preheat oven to 350 degrees. Saute onion in butter. Add meat, parsley and spices. Shred cabbage and place half in the casserole. Add meat mixture. Place remaining cabbage in the casserole. Pour the soup on top. Cover. Bake 1 hour.

Turk Tangert
Lancaster, Pennsylvania

Antelope Chili

Serves: 6
Prep Time: overnight

2 lbs. antelope, diced
1 T. bacon drippings
2 T. chili powder
1 tsp. sage
1 tsp. ground black pepper
1 tsp. salt
1 tsp. ground cumin
½ tsp. cayenne pepper
1 carrot, diced
2 onions, diced
2 cloves garlic, diced
1 quart canned tomatoes
2 cups water
¼ cup pinto beans

Wash pinto beans. Soak overnight in 3 cups water. Cook 1 hour. In non-stick skillet, lightly brown antelope in bacon drippings. Drain. Add chili powder, sage, black pepper, salt, cumin, cayenne pepper, onion, garlic. Stir well. In a large heavy pot, add this to tomatoes, carrots and water. Bring to boil. Reduce heat, cover and simmer for 1 hour. Add pinto beans and cook 1 additional hour. Serve with corn bread.

Robert Parker
Las Vegas, Nevada

Waterfowl

Baked Wild Duck

Serves: 3-4
Prep Time: 2½ hours

   1 **duck**
      salt and pepper
1-2 **onions**
   1 **bell pepper**
   3 **celery sticks**
   1 **orange**
  ½ **cup wine**
      vinegar water

Soak bird in vinegar water for 1 hour to remove gamey taste. Salt and pepper inside and outside of bird generously. Stuff bird with peeled orange (keep peels), chopped celery, chopped bell pepper and chopped onion. Place bird in Dutch oven, put orange peels on top. Bake, covered at 350 degrees for 1 hour. Pour wine over bird and bake for an additional ½ hour.

Brian Giles
San Angelo, Texas

Duck Un Kraut

Serves: 2
Prep Time: 45 minutes

- 1 **duck**
- 2 **quarts sauerkraut**
- 1 **cup water**
- 3 **T. sugar**
  salt and pepper

Prepare a young duck for roasting. Place in a roasting pan and add sauerkraut, water and sugar. Cover and bake until golden brown and tender. Serve with creamy buttered potatoes.

Dave Hepler
Monroe, Utah

Bristol Bay Goose

Serves: 2-4
Prep Time: 2 hours

- 1 **good size Emperor goose**
- ½ **cup flour**
- ½ **cup bread crumbs**
- 1 **tsp. salt**
- ½ **tsp. pepper**
- 2 **diced onions**
  cooking oil
- 2 **T. lemon juice**
- 1 **tsp. garlic powder**
- 1 **tsp. paprika**

Cut up goose and soak in cold water for 1 hour. Roll the pieces in a mixture of flour, bread crumbs, salt, pepper and garlic powder. Brown the goose in 5 T. cooking oil and add the onions and lemon juice. Sprinkle on paprika. Cover and cook until tender.

"Alaska" Rick Sinchak
Warren, Ohio

Wild Goose

Serves: 2-4
Prep Time: 2 hours

2½ quarts stale bread, broken up
goose giblets, diced
1 lg. onion, chopped
2 Jonathan apples, diced
sage, garlic
salt and pepper

Clean and pick the goose well. Do not skin. Boil the giblets until tender, then dice. Combine giblets with bread, apples and onion. Add salt and pepper, sage and garlic. Moisten and stuff the goose. Place goose in roasting pan and spread with 2 T. butter. Cook at 350 degrees until done, about 15 to 20 minutes per pound. Baste often.

Marge Schultz
Bronson, Kansas

Booger Woods Goose

Serves: 2-4
Prep Time: 4 hours

  1 **goose**
  ½ **cup celery, chopped**
  ½ **cup onion, chopped**
  1 **lb. scrapple**
  6 **slices bread**
  1 **egg**
  1 **tsp. poultry seasoning**
  ½ **cup milk**
     salt, pepper, garlic, paprika

     Glaze:
  ½ **cup honey**
  3 **T. BBQ sauce**
  4 **T. orange marmalade**
  1 **tsp. black pepper**

Soak goose for 1 hour in cold water and 3 T. salt. Combine celery, onion, scrapple, bread, egg, poultry seasoning and milk in large bowl. Salt and pepper to taste. Remove goose from water and pat dry. Stuff goose with above ingredients. Place in roasting pan with ¼ cup water. Combine glaze ingredients and brush on goose. Sprinkle paprika and garlic over goose to taste. Cover and place in oven at 350 degrees for 2 hours. Every ½ hour remove goose and brush on glaze until thick coating covers goose.

John Alex Paxson
Philadelphia, Pennsylvania

New Friends

by
CHARLES L. BRIDWELL

Often, the worst part of moving to a new home is not the moving itself, but rather the things that are left behind. Neighbors, friends, family, church, even the house all have special meaning to us, and with them we leave a portion of ourselves.

Among the most difficult things in life to part with is a hunting partner. It sometimes takes years of hunting together to attain that special understanding that only hunting buddies share. You know each other's faults and good points. You know you can count on him to be at your house at the appointed time with all his gear. You've found that he is an ethical sportsman, careful with his weapon and considerate of others. He always pays his way, doesn't bum your food, and if he says "I'll take my truck next time," he really will. He doesn't try to get the first shot, give commands to your dog or talk about his marital problems. And most of all, he doesn't have to kill a thing to have a great day afield.

I recently moved from one side of the state to another and experienced first hand the agonies of moving, along with the heartbreak of leaving some good hunting buddies behind. I tried to ease the discomfort by going back to hunt with them, but I quickly saw that it was costing me more to drive back and forth than it was to actually pursue the sport. As much as I hated to admit it, I had to find a new partner.

It was already October when I started my search. I began going to gun shops and other sportsmen's hangouts to see if I might locate someone who would fill the bill. It takes a special person to be a hunting partner, and even more special to be a duck hunter. I found out anew that duck hunters are a reclusive bunch, though not quite as bad as turkey hunters. Everyone I talked to said they didn't even know anyone who duck hunted, and they didn't believe there were any ducks around here anyway. I knew better. I was being "snowed."

Since I couldn't find someone who was willing to work me into their happy hunting ground, I realized I would have to start someone totally green, a pup, so to speak, and train them from the very beginning. It wouldn't be easy.

I met Mike at church. A tall, gangling fellow of about 20 years, he seemed like a nice enough chap. In the course of our conversation, he told me he was an avid deer hunter. I, of course, told him about duck hunting. Mike said that he had never tried it, but would like to some time. I told him he would have to get some waders and some warm clothes, buy the required duck stamps, and get some shot at least size six or larger.

Most folks change their minds pretty fast about duck hunting when you explain to them what they have to have and they realize the type of weather that must be endured. I figured that Mike, just as so many others, would decide he already had enough hunting sports without adding another that was as demanding as duck hunting.

To my surprise, the following week Mike asked me when I was going to take him hunting. He had already borrowed some waders, and bought his shells and duck stamps. I shouldn't have been surprised at all. If I had only remembered myself at his age, I would have recalled the youthful enthusiasm that let me rush into any new sport without a second thought as to the cost. I set the date for us to make our first trip and could almost feel his excitement as he said; "Just tell me the time and I'll be there!"

I'd like to say that we went on our first hunt together and had a great day. It would make a great tale to say that the ducks worked to our decoys like sailors home from the sea and that we both limited out. That would be, at the least, a

gross fabrication. Truth is, we walked about two miles through flooded timber carrying a dozen decoys each and got cold, wet, tired and even a little lost. Worst of all, Mike didn't even get a shot at a duck.

As we drove home, Mike didn't have much to say. When he finally spoke, it made me realize that I had found someone with the potential to become a good partner. "You know what?" he said, "I think I'm really gonna' like this duck hunting. It's not like any other hunting I've ever done. I think it's the *ifs* that make it so interesting."

I had to find out what he meant, so I shot back "What do you mean, the *ifs*."

"Well, it's like this," he said, "You can only have a successful duck hunt *if* everything comes together just right. *If* there are plenty of ducks, *if* you can fool them with good calling and realistic decoys, and *if* you can shoot well when and *if* they decide to come in!

I was dumfounded! Here was a first timer telling me he had enjoyed the hunt because it was so unpredictable, because we had worked so hard and still came home empty handed! I realized at once that he was right. Those were precisely the reasons I kept hunting. The effort and sacrifice are all justified when everything works just right.

You might say I redeemed myself on our next hunt. Like before, Mike arrived bright-eyed and eager, a full 20 minutes before I had told him to be at my house. He had the boat loaded and ready to go long before I had finished the first of the required three cups of coffee. Even though our last hunt had been a washout, I had a feeling that today would be different. We were the first hunters to the boat ramp.

Thirty minutes later we were deep in the flooded bottomlands of the Bois D' Arc Wildlife Management Area in southwest Arkansas. We had no sooner set up, when ducks began flying in the pre-dawn light. Mike was wiggling like a pointer pup as he leaned against a great oak heavy with acorns. He watched the dark skies with anticipation, straining to see the ducks whistling overhead. As eager as he was, Mike still wasn't prepared for the green-winged teal that appeared out of the mist. He came in low, only a couple of feet above the water.

At Mike's first shot, the teal pulled straight up and climbed like a rocket. Mike's follow up shots were as ineffective as the first. Almost as an afterthought, I swung the muzzle of my old pump upwards until the duck disappeared and let loose a charge of handloaded sixes. I tried to remain nonchalant as the teal folded, and plummeted to the water. "This is as it should be," I thought as I waded out to my prize. "Me, the old expert, finishing what the youngster had started."

The next duck to come in was a mallard drake that fell into the "dekes" like a rock dropped from some unseen airplane. I had no time to even think about telling Mike to shoot. He hadn't even seen the duck until I shot. The shot was as sure as it was quick, and I was feeling pretty smug as I waded out after my second duck. Two for two is not bad in a duck marsh. I should have known it would not last.

Mike saw the bluebills first and said "Hey, what kind of ducks were those?" I informed him that they were scaup, and that if they came close enough for a shot, we'd have to lead them plenty and keep swinging. On their next pass, we were both embarrassed as they passed within 25 yards of us and we both shot three times without so much as ruffling a

feather.

Shortly thereafter, a pair of fat mallard drakes came a little too close, and Mike got them both with three shots. I was elated. This is what I had intended for him from the first, and now he was seeing what duck hunting really was like. From then on, the day just seemed to melt into a dream. Many ducks flew over our decoys before we called it a day. Some left a little smarter, and some of them joined our bag to become the main ingredient for my famous duck gumbo. I would have been content for it to have ended there. I had no way of knowing that my greatest all-time duck hunting thrill in already heading my way from out of the Northern skies.

At first, I thought they were blackbirds because mallards don't usually fly in flocks of 40 birds in the middle of the day, at least not in this area. But as they approached closer, my heart thumped in my chest as I realized that they were really ducks, and headed our way. These weren't ordinary ducks, they were flight ducks, those weary travelers from the North just aching to find a place of rest and solitude. My hands trembled as I reached for my call.

I was so excited I could hardly blow it and was afraid that one wrong note would send them on their way. They came directly overhead, still high enough to see Texas. I suggested, then pleaded, then begged them to come down and pay us a brief visit. They finally swung around and began that slow circling descent that seems to take forever. They finally cupped their wings in one accord and headed in low over the decoys. Those green heads and orange legs looked so gaudy against the cloudless blue sky. They were talking among themselves, wondering if they should take the time to drop in on their fake cousins below. I made those happy little feeding sounds the best I could with my heart doing the boogie woogie in my chest.

"Don't shoot!" I whispered to Mike. It seemed that surely the ducks could hear our breathing they were so close, but I wanted to light this bunch. It was a gamble, but it paid off. They made one short circle and landed right smack dab in the middle of our decoys. The instant we moved it seemed the world was full of wings and quacks. It didn't last long, but the scene will be printed on my mind forever. Mike and I both waded out after the ducks that would fill our limits, both in mild shock, too stunned by the beauty of the moment to ruin it with conversation. It's something I'll remember as long as I live.

Mike won't soon forget it either. In fact, he hasn't stopped talking about it since. He brought me a cap the other day with a big mallard drake painted on the front. "I know this isn't much," he said, "but I want to give it to you as an appreciation gift for taking the time and effort to break me in. I never thought I would find anything I like as much as I

like duck hunting, thanks to you." He showed me the new duck call he had bought and asked me to tune it for him and show him how to blow it so he could help me with the calling chores next year. We talked of decoys, hunting gear and all the other hunts we had this past season. But there was a certain amount of reverence when we spoke of the "big bunch" that made the brief stop in our spread before heading on to the South.

Of course I had to kid Mike a little bit before he left. You see, I didn't tell you about his getting stuck on the boat ramp, or when he let us run out of gas deep in the bottoms, or the time he forgot the plug for the boat..., well, you understand. Breaking in a partner is tough. They're green at first, and it takes time to show them all the ropes. Their questions must be answered with patience. It takes patience too, when they shoot a 100-point duck the first thing. An investment must be made in them, an investment of time, patience and most of all, self. That's why it's so difficult to break in a new partner, and why it's so very hard to leave a good one behind.

Small game

ANDERSON

Woodlot Squirrel

Serves: 4
Prep Time: 1 hour

- **3 squirrels**
- **1 egg**
  bread crumbs
- **2 T. butter**
- **2 T. oil**
  pepper
- **½ cup white wine**
- **½ cup orange juice**

Dry squirrel. Beat egg. Add garlic and onion salt to crumbs.
Dip squirrel in egg, then dry mixture. Brown squirrel in butter
or oil and add white wine and juice. Cover and simmer 45
minutes to 1 hour, turn once during cooking.

Warna Reed
Matherville, Illinois

Casserole of Squirrel

Serves: 4
Prep Time: 1¼ hours

> 2 squirrels
> seasoned flour
> ¼ cup rice
> 2 green peppers, diced
> 1½ cup celery, diced
> 1 cup tart apple slices
> boiling water

Disjoint the squirrels, roll in seasoned flour. Arrange in a
well-greased casserole dish. Sprinkle with rice, peppers,
celery and apples. Cover with boiling water and bake,
tightly covered, for 1 hour at 300 degrees or until tender.

Jim Kemp
Charlestown, Indiana

Tundra Hare

Serves: 2-4
Prep Time: overnight

> 1 hare, cut into small pieces
> 1½ cups vinegar
> 1 cup water
> ½ cup flour
> salt and pepper
> 1 tsp. onion powder

Cut hare into small pieces and sprinkle onion powder over
them. Place in a bowl and add the water and vinegar. Let
stand overnight. The next morning, put the contents in a pot
and cook until tender. Add flour to thicken. Serve with hot
biscuits.

"Alaska" Rick Sinchak
Warren, Ohio

Squabbit

Serves: 4-6
Prep Time: 1½ hours

- **3 squirrels, quartered**
- **3 rabbits, quartered**
- **½ cup wine vinegar**
- **1 tsp. garlic salt**
- **½ tsp. rosemary**
- **½ tsp. oregano**
- **1 bay leaf**
  salt and pepper
- **¼ cup celery, diced**
- **1 med. onion, diced**
- **2 T. butter**
- **2 med. potatoes, cubed**
- **1 cup peas, frozen or fresh**
- **1 cup mushrooms, sliced**
- **1 can cream of mushroom soup**
- **1 envelope homestyle gravy mix**
- **½ cup red wine**

In Dutch oven, place meat and vinegar, cover with water. Bring to a boil and simmer 15 minutes. Drain and remove meat. In the same pan, saute onion and celery in butter. Add garlic salt, rosemary, oregano, bay leaf, salt, pepper and meat. Cover with water and simmer until tender. Remove meat from the bones and return to pit. Add remaining ingredients, stir and simmer until potatoes are done.

Any small game or upland birds could be substituted. To shorten preparation time, potatoes could be eliminated and the dish served over toast, egg noodles or rice.

Harry Covert
New City, New York

Rabbit Super-ize

Serves: 4
Prep Time: 1 1/2 hours

> 2 **rabbits**
>   **meat tenderizer**
> 3-4 **cloves of garlic**
> 1 **small sliced tomato**
> 3 **onions**
> ¼ **cup pepper sauce**
> ¼ **cup red vinegar**
> ¼ **cup real lemon juice**
>   **sprinkle of salt to taste**

Cut rabbits into bite size pieces. Fry for ten minutes until brown. Then put in your seasonings. Sprinkle some meat tenderizer over all parts of the meat. Put in one cup of water and stir.

Lay some garlic around the meat. Slice in one whole tomato. Cut up the onions over the meat. Put in ½ cup of pepper sauce, homemade is best. Stir all of this in, around and over meat. Then add ¼ cup lemon juice and salt meat lightly. Cover with lid and cook over low heat. Allow to simmer until well done.

Pour your favorite smoked barbecue sauce over the meat and serve.

Glover Roston, Sr.
Cleveland Heights, Ohio

Hassenpfeffer

Serves: 2
Prep Time: 4½ hours

- 1 **rabbit, quartered**
- ½ **cup Kosher salt**
- 1 **cup wine vinegar**
- ½ **cup brown sugar**
- ½ **cup tomato sauce**
- 1 **cup flour**
- 1 **quart water**
- 1 **cup water**
- ½ **onion, sliced**
- 3 **carrots**
- 1 **oz. butter**

Soak rabbit for 2-3 hours in water and Kosher salt. Discard water and salt. Combine wine vinegar, water, brown sugar, onion and tomato sauce. Marinate rabbit for 30 minutes. Remove rabbit and dredge in flour. Brown in large skillet. After browning, add enough marinade to cover. Peel carrots and slice into skillet. Simmer until rabbit and carrots are tender, about 1 hour. Serve with hot biscuits.

Milton Raynor
Eastport, New York

Rabbit Pie

Serves: 4
Prep Time: 1 hour

- 1 **rabbit**
  water
  salt
- 3 **T. butter**
- 3 **T. onion, chopped**
- 3 **T. parsley, minced**
  flour
  Tabasco

Cut the rabbit into 3 or 4 pieces. Place in a sauce pan and barely cover with water. Cover the pan and simmer until tender. Add salt to season when partially cooked. Drain and measure the liquid. Remove the meat from the bones, keeping it in large pieces. Heat 3 T. butter in a skillet, add onion and parsley. Cook about 5 minutes, stirring constantly. Use 1½ T. flour to each cup of liquid and mix well in the skillet with the onion. Stir until mixture thickens. Add more salt if needed and a dash of Tabasco. Add meat to mixture and pour into a baking dish. Cover with pastry and bake at 350 degrees for 35 minutes.

Dave Hepler
Monroe, Utah

Upland bird

Pheasant Cream Soup

Serves: 6
Prep Time: 1¼ hours

- **2 quarts hot water**
- **1 pheasant, sectioned**
- **6 chicken bouillon cubes**
- **¼ tsp. paprika**
- **1 tsp. poultry seasoning**
  salt and pepper
- **2 T. cornstarch**
- **½ cup water**

Combine 2 quarts water, pheasant pieces and bouillon cubes in pot. Simmer 50 minutes or until tender. Remove pheasant, cool and debone meat. Pour broth through a strainer into a large mixing bowl. Discard strainer contents. Return meat and broth to original cooking pot. Add paprika, poultry seasoning, salt and pepper. Bring soup to a low boil. Dissolve cornstarch in ½ cup water. Stirring constantly, add cornstarch mixture to soup. Stir until soup has thickened, about 5 minutes. Serve hot.

Marge Schultz
Bronson, Kansas

Tasty Fried Pheasant

Serves: 4-5
Prep Time: 2 hours

  1 **pheasant**
1-2 **cups buttermilk**
    flour to coat
    cooking oil

Remove bone from pheasant. Slice into thin strips. Soak in buttermilk for 1 ½ to 2 hours. Remove and dip strips in flour. Fry in hot oil until golden brown. Drain on paper towel.

Bob Dinsdale
Sugar Creek, Missouri

Pheasant Patties

Serves: 2-4
Prep Time: 1 hour

    ground pheasant meat
    egg
    salt and pepper
    dried bread crumbs
    oil
    cream of mushroom soup

Use pheasant meat from legs and breasts which have been torn or shot up too much to keep whole, and grind it. Form meat into patties. Dip patties into beaten egg, season with salt and pepper and roll in bread crumbs. Fry in oil for about 20 to 30 minutes on low heat. Or, you can place patties in a casserole dish and pour cream of chicken or mushroom soup over and bake at 350 degrees for 1 hour.

Mrs. Ken Reuter
Humboldt, South Dakota

Joe Martin's Herb Roasted Pheasant

Serves: 4
Prep Time: 1 1/2 hours

- 1 **plucked pheasant**
- 1½ **cups cooked wild rice**
- ¼ **cup celery**
- ¼ **cup onion**
- ⅔ **cup butter or margarine**
- ½ **tsp. thyme**
- ½ **tsp. garlic powder**
- 1 **tsp. rosemary**
  salt and pepper to taste

Wash pheasant inside and out. Pat dry with paper towels. Prepare rice and set aside. Saute onion and celery until tender, about 5 minutes. Stuff pheasant making sure it's not too full. Stitch closed with poultry skewers. Preheat oven to 350 degrees.
Melt butter and add rosemary, thyme and garlic powder. Baste the bird several times during cooking. Place bird in roasting pan and cook 60 to 75 minutes until bird is nicely browned and drumsticks move easily.

Joseph M. Martin
Fremont, California

Barbeque Dove

Serves: 4
Prep Time: 40 minutes

- **16 dove breasts**
- **1 lb. bacon**
- **1 bottle barbeque sauce**
- **salt and pepper**
- **16 toothpicks**

Salt and pepper dove breasts. Wrap ¾ piece of bacon around each breast and hold with toothpick. Put doves on grill about 10 inches above coals. Cook slowly on both sides, approximately 15 minutes per side. Remove bacon and add barbeque sauce. Leave on grill with breast facing up for another 10 minutes.

Jeff Atteberry
Urbana, Missouri

Smoked Yard Birds

Serves: 6-8
Prep Time: 24 hours

- 1 **turkey or partridge**
- 1 **cup Morton's Tender Quick Salt**
- 1 **gallon water**
- 1 **cup brown sugar**
- 1 **T. Lawry's Seasoned Salt**
- 1 **pinch garlic powder**

Mix all ingredients. Put bird in mixture, cover and refrigerate for 10 hours. Smoke in smoker for 8 hours using apple wood or maple wood chips.

Orrin Sandy
Pentwater, Michigan

Gloria's Wild Bird Stuffing

Serves: a large group
Prep Time: 1 1/2 hours

- 15 cups dried bread crumbs
- 2 sticks butter or margarine
- 1 egg, beaten
- ½ tsp. sage
- ⅛ tsp. paprika
- 1 T. salt
- ½ T. black pepper
- 1 cup chopped yellow onion
- 2 cups chopped celery
- ½ cup finely chopped red apples
- 1 cube chicken bouillon
- 5 cups water

Dry 60 slices of bread overnight. Crumble in large bowl. In a sauce pan, melt butter. Saute onion and celery until almost clear. Dissolve bouillon cube in hot water and let cool. Mix all ingredients in bowl with bread crumbs. Spoon mixture into bird's cavity. Any leftover can be baked in a greased oven dish or roasting pan for about an hour.

Terry Swenson
Maple Grove, Minnesota

Gobbler a la Mojo

Serves: a family
Prep Time: 4 hours or so

- 1 **wild turkey (ready to cook)**
- 1 **stick butter**
- **salt**
- **black pepper**
- **flour**
- **water**

Remove neck and giblets from turkey and set aside. Melt butter and brush on turkey. Sprinkle inside and out with salt and black pepper. Stuff cavity with your favorite dressing and sew shut. Tuck drumsticks under bird and fold wings to body. If bird is large, (older than a jake), wrap completely with foil before placing in roasting pan. This will keep the bird moist and preserve the tenderness and delicate wild flavor. Cook in 400 degree oven for 15-20 minutes per pound. About 45 minutes before done, begin basting with juices. You can also baste with melted butter. If using a meat thermometer, bird is done when dial reads 185 degrees. Turkey should cool about 20 minutes before carving. While the bird is cooking, finely chop giblets and boil in lightly salted water with neck. Simmer until giblets are tender. Discard neck. Add cold water to 6 tablespoons flour to make paste. Bring stock to a boil and slowly add flour to mixture. For added flavor, add a few spoonfuls of dripping from turkey pan. Stir constantly until desired thickness. Salt and pepper to taste, you've got gravy!

Bob Collins
Minneapolis, Minnesota

Missouri Woodcocks

Serves: 2-4
Prep Time: ½ hour

- 5 whole woodcocks
- 1 cup flour
- ½ tsp. ground peppercorns
- ½ tsp. paprika
  salt to taste
- ⅔ cup bacon drippings
- 1 T. butter
- ⅔ cup dry white wine

Roll meat in flour seasoned with pepper, paprika and salt.
Brown in bacon drippings, then drain meat and pour off
drippings, wipe skillet. Return meat to skillet, add butter and
wine, simmer gently for 10 minutes.

Jim Cobb
Rolla, Missouri

Barbequed Sage Hen

Serves: 4-5
Prep Time: 4 hours

2 sage hens, cut up
2 cups milk
   barbeque sauce

Soak sage hens in milk for 2 to 3 hours. Drain. Put on grill and cook until almost done. Brush with barbeque sauce and cook until done.

Russell Collins
Dubois, Wyoming

Lloyd's Quail Delight

Serves: 4-5
Prep Time: 1 ½ hours

7-9 quail
  6 carrots, sliced
  3 green peppers, sliced
  6 stalks celery, sliced
  2 large onions, diced
  1 tsp. salt
 ¼ tsp. pepper
 ¼ cup flour
 ⅓ cup white cooking wine
     butter

Mix salt, pepper and flour and place in a paper bag. Place 3 quail at a time in bag and shake well. Brown quail in a large skillet with butter. Add wine by pouring over the quail. Add onions, celery, carrots and green peppers. Cover skillet and simmer for 1 hour.

R. Scott Lloyd
Hernando, Mississippi

Dove Lessons

by
RICK BASS

We drove all night. My little brother liked that. It was an adventure in itself. The windows down, we just rolled along the highway under cool cover of the darkness—stars out, radio on louder than Mom ever let us play it. We felt an unquestioned permission to act natural.

We talked about school, about his gym teacher, about astronauts and rodeo horses. We stopped at the Sonic Drive-In in Shreveport and had strawberry milkshakes and french fries. And I didn't make him finish his cheeseburger.

We were headed for Texas and opening day of the South Zone dove season. With his other brothers off at college and Dad working out of town, BJ thought he wasn't going to get to go. He'd been practicing with the .410 for two months. In the truck he told me, with a nine-year-old's going-to-Texas-with-the-windows-down, eating-what-I-want braggadocio, that he had gotten quite deadly with the little gun. That was what I wanted to hear.

"There's gonna be lots of bird flying," I said. In my minds eye I could see them. They had to be there. It was going to be opening day. "we're going to kill us some birds BJ Bass," I assured him, slapping him on the knee and grinning.

He grinned back and took a swig of milk shake. "Oh boy," he said then, as if remembering something, corrected it. "Hot damn," he said.

My jaw dropped open; I tried to look stern and disapproving, but couldn't. We both laughed. I nodded. "Hot damn is right," I said. "Hot damn!"

We hit Uvalde, Texas at one in the morning and checked into the Holiday Inn. Camouflaged jeeps and old pick-up trucks sat dark and silent in the parking lot. We had come to the right place. We struggled with the room key, got it to open and trudged inside.

"Cable TV," BJ cried and watched a satellite replay of U.C.L.A. and Georgia. It was like being grown up for him and a kid for me. We were having a wonderful time!

We put the guns up and had a pillow fight. Then we had wars with the flyswatter. We talked. I told him a little about dove hunting, why you have to wear camouflage and what doves eat. Then I read for awhile. When he fell asleep, suddenly exhausted, I pulled his boots off and let him sleep just as he was—still in his clothes, arms awkwardly askew—the way kids sleep when they are really tired. I didn't know what time it was, but I really didn't care. I was on vacation. Our wake-up call would come at 10:00.

The Bass lease is a small one, only 200 acres, but just right for two brothers, one of them young and used to taking short steps. BJ had to walk with me. No way was I going to let him off by himself. He'd learned a lot, but it was just one of those things. I could get more doves with him up the creek and me down, but that's not what this hunt was for.

"Oh boy," he said when I told him we were going to walk the sunflowers together. His face was already shiny. He was already sweating like a bandit. We were both decked out in the dove hunter's traditional camo. He even insisted on wearing it to breakfast.

143

By 2:00 p.m. we'd had no luck. We jumped about four doves, but all too far away to shoot. BJ was kicking rocks; not on purpose, but I was still amazed. His foot seemed like a magnet for them. I weigh 175 pounds; he weighs at best, 55. How was it that I could walk so much more quietly? I scowled and explained to him that he must walk more quietly. He nodded, and we continued on. He flanked me, a little behind and to the left, barrel pointed still further left, the way I taught him. But he still crunched sticks and booted rocks, though he studied intently where to place each step.

A bird jumped to his left making that unmistakable cut-flutter whistling of wings. I went temporarily hyper, for a flash of a second, but caught myself. With great effort I remained calm.

"You've got to watch the fields," I told him objectively, neutrally. "That was your bird. You can't be watching the ground. They'll jump up and be gone before you can shoot them." I spoke more calmly than I ever had before; too calmly because he nodded as nonchalantly as I had spoken. It was no big deal to him.

"Don't let them get away," I told him, still somewhat matter of factly and he nodded again. He still watched the ground as he walked, picking his steps. Still hitting the same rocks, but picking them now.

We left the field and went back to the truck for a break, a rest in the shade, a soda pop and a coldcuts and cheese sandwich. He like that. We sat under a big oak, one of the few in that country. We weren't seeing any doves; we weren't pursuing any, but we were happy. We finished our sandwiches and the last of our drinks, and I got up.

Dutifully, BJ rose to his feet too.

We moved up into the tall grass on the level at the end of the little creek where there was a stock tank for long-ago cattle. Deer, raccoons, coyotes and other desert-scrub animals use it now. We sat in the grass awhile, under a tiny mesquite, and waited. The sun was tough—107, 108 degrees. It was 3:00 p.m. and overpowering. You had to be strong or it would just knock you down. Moving around in it was like walking with an unbalanced and very heavy load on your back. I noticed that BJ was not crouched scanning the skies, but instead was abstractly studying the tops of his boots. I said nothing. At least he was camouflaged well.

A great green bullfrog the color of an olive, the size of a large stone popped to the surface of the stock tank and looked speculatively at us. I pointed him out to BJ.

"We could shoot him!" he said eagerly. I wondered if I had trained the blood lust too strong in this one. Was the frog to be his revenge for the non-appearing doves?

"What would we do this evening then?" I asked, thinking of walking back to the truck in warm South Texas twilight and listening to the deep and mystical summertime drumming.

"Eat him?" BJ suggested hopefully, shifting his gun a little. But I explained how important frogs are in little ponds like that one, and how nice they sound in the evening. He considered it all and looked at the frog again. I could tell he was looking differently, maybe still wanting to shoot it, but at least looking at it in a new way, with a new angle.

An hour later there were still no birds.

"I need to stretch," he whispered. I nodded permission, and of course as he stood up a bird flew over—or started to anyway. It saw BJ and flared. BJ fired and missed. My criticism was overly sharp. "You've got to always look around before you stand up!" I snapped. "To see if any of them are coming like that!" His face fell and he sat back down without stretching. He watched the sky anxiously, I think hoping that by spotting a bird he could make up for his transgression.

Sure, he learned, he'd remember next time to look up first, but I still felt bad. Surely I could have taught him just as effectively without being harsh. Anyway, it was a little thing, forgotten quickly when another bird, miracle of miracles, did fly over, and I rose up and shot him. Feathers puffed and he tumbled into the reeds along the tank's edge. It was a good feeling, a wonderful one—my little brother seeing me rise up out of the grass like that and dropping the fast-flying dove with a beautiful shot as if it was nothing, as if there were never any doubt.

An hour later we were still looking for the bird. To me it had only been an hour. To him it had been eternities. At any rate, the lesson had been learned.

It was past time. We had tried and then some. We were

missing out on the best part of the hunt, the best time of the day—the evening. We turned to leave, to sit under the mesquite again, and I found the bird. Inside my heart was leaping; I felt wonderful, but I just nodded curtly as if there had never been any doubt. It is bad for a student not to have confidence in his teacher.

We started back up the levee over the little stock tank. I watched him closely. He was not watching the sky. He was dragging.

We crested the levee and continued on down into the mesquite/oak creekbottom behind it. When doves jumped up out of the trees, I told him to shoot them. He did—or tried anyway—and missed. I grinned and said "You clipped him! I saw a feather fly!" And he said, grinning and kind of excited, "Yeah, I clipped him anyway!" Then I pointed out an Indian arrowhead sticking half out of the dirt. I told him Indians used to live here and realized he was more interested than he had been all weekend.

We set our guns aside and hunted arrowheads 'til dark.

Miscellaneous

Junjik River Dall Roast

Serves: 4-6
Prep Time: 2 hours

- 1 **thick slab of ram**
- 5 **tsp. bacon fat**
- ½ **tsp. pepper**
- 1 **T. parsley, chopped**
- ½ **cup flour**
- ½ **cup corn meal**
- 1 **tsp. salt**
- 2 **T. onion, chopped**
- 3 **cups boiling water**

Put the slab on a board and pound the flour and corn meal into it. Melt the fat in a large frying pan and brown the roast. Add all of the seasoning and about ½ the boiling water. Cover and let simmer for about 1 hour. Then add the rest of the water and simmer again until tender.

"Alaska" Rick Sinchak
Warren, Ohio

Buffalo Medallions

Serves: 2
Prep Time: ½ hour

4 2 oz. buffalo medallions cut from the tenderloin
1 T. butter
1 jigger Jack Daniels whiskey
¼ cup reduced veal stock
2 tsp. heavy cream
salt and pepper

In a small skillet, melt butter until it turns light brown. Reduce heat and saute the medallions on both sides for 3 to 4 minutes or until done to your taste. Place medallions on a preheated plate. Discard the butter in which the medallions were cooked. Place skillet back on the heat and deglaze with Jack Daniels. Immediately add veal stock and reduce to half over medium heat. Add cream, stir well and season to taste. Spoon sauce on plate and top with medallions.

Marge Schultz
Bronson, Kansas

Baked Coon

Serves: 4-6
Prep Time: 2 hours

1 **coon**
12 **potatoes**
1 **med. onion**
3 **med. carrots**
Worcestershire
salt and pepper
1 **cup water**

Cook coon in a pot of water until meat falls off bones. Line baking pan with foil. Debone coon, put in pan with potatoes, onions, carrots, water, Worcestershire, salt and pepper. Bake at 350 degrees until potatoes are done.

Jessica McNeese
Tylertown, Mississippi

Breaded Brain

Serves: 2
Prep Time: overnight

> **brain from large game animal**
> **egg**
> **cracker crumbs**
> **bacon drippings**

Salt the brain lightly and refrigerate overnight. When ready to prepare, dip brain in hot water to remove the outer membrane, which will peel off easily. Dip brain pieces in beaten egg, roll in cracker crumbs and fry in bacon drippings. Season with salt and pepper.

Carl Allen
Cincinnati, Ohio

Fried Heart

Serves: 2
Prep Time: 45 minutes

> 1 **game heart**
> ½ **cup flour**
> **salt and pepper**
> 2 **T. bacon grease**
> 2 **cups hot water**
> 1 **tsp. oregano**

Dice heart into pieces not more than ½-inch thick. Place flour in a paper bag, add meat, salt and pepper and shake to coat. Fry in bacon grease until well seared, add water and oregano and cook slowly, uncovered for ½ hour.

Carl Allen
Cincinnati, Ohio

Ground Hogs

Serves: 6-8
Prep Time: 2½-3 hours

2 **Ground hogs**
½ **tsp. salt**
2-3 **T. pepper**
3 **onions**
6-8 **potatoes**
4-5 **carrots, sliced**

Boil ground hog until tender. Remove from water and debone. Sprinkle completely with pepper. Slice oinons, potatoes and carrots. Add to meat and bake at 375 degrees until well browned. Also good for raccoon.

James Adkins Jr.
Richmond, Kentucky

Wild Buzztail Rice

Serves: 4
Prep Time: 1½ hours

1-2 **large buzztails**
1 **box Uncle Ben's Wild Rice**
garlic
2 **T. butter**
soy sauce
1 **T. salt**

Boil snakes for approximately 1 hour in saltwater until tender. Debone. Saute meat in garlic and butter 5-10 minutes. Prepare rice per instructions on box. Mix meat and rice. Add soy sauce to taste.

M.R. Moore
Huffman, Texas

Wild Boar Stew

Serves: 6
Prep Time: 4 hours

2-3 lbs. wild boar
  2 lbs. potatoes
  2 onions
  3 stalks celery
  3 large carrots
  1 16 oz. can corn, drained
  1 10 oz. can tomato sauce
  1 10 oz. can beef broth
¼ tsp. sage
¼ tsp. curry powder
  dash of Tabasco

Peel and dice potatoes and onions. Dice celery and carrots.
Cut boar meat into ½-inch cubes. Add to crockpot with
remaining ingredients. Cook in pot on high for 3½-4 hours or
until meat is tender. Stir occasionally.

Fred Evans
Miramar, Florida

Fox Nuggets

Serves: 2-4
Prep Time: overnight

- **1 fox**
- **1 onion, chopped**
- **3 cloves garlic, minced**
- **½ cup red wine vingear**
- **2 T. sugar**
- **⅓ cup Mesquite or Hickory smoke flavor cooking oil**

Skin, debone and cut fox meat into strips about 2-3 inches long, removing most of the fat and tendons. Mix all of the above ingredients except oil in a one-gallon Zip-lock plastic bag. Close the bag and kneed the contents to cover the fox well. Place the bag in the refrigerator for at least 10 hours or overnight, turning once or twice. The next day, heat the oil to 350 degrees while draining the meat in a colander, discarding the marinade. Deep fry the meat about 3-5 minutes or until well done. Drain on paper towel. Serve with any dipping sauce if you prefer, but they are good plain as well.

Anthony Vernier
Allegan, Michigan

Darrel's Fried Turtle

Serves: 4
Prep Time: 3 1/2 hours

> 1 **large snapping turtle (cleaned and cut into
>   pieces)**
>   **flour**
> 3 **large cloves of garlic**

Fry floured turtle in one inch of oil until all sides are a golden
brown. Remove turtle when seared, then take out some of
the oil. Replace all of turtle into remaining oil and add a
little water. Throw chopped garlic on top. Simmer for 3½
hours adding water as necessary.

Darrel F. Glaser
Spring Grove, Illinois

Legs 'n' Eggs

Serves: 4
Prep Time: 20 minutes

  6 **large eggs**
12 **hind legs from Leopard or Bull frogs**
¼ **cup onion, chopped**
¼ **cup green chile, chopped**
½ **cup cheese, grated**
    salt
    pepper
    paprika
  2 **T. oil**

Skin legs and cut meat off of bone. Cube meat into small pieces and rinse in cold water. Add a dash of salt, pepper and paprika. Heat oil in a skillet. Saute onions until tender, add meat from frog legs and brown lightly. Break eggs into pan, stirring constantly and add green chile. Remove pan from heat, sprinkle grated cheese on top. Serve hot.

Linda Locklar
Silver City, New Mexico

Cajun Frog Legs

Serves: 4
Prep Time: 30 minutes

12 frog legs
3 eggs
12 oz. seasoned bread crumbs
1 tsp. yellow mustard
juice of 1 lemon
salt
pepper
1 T. cayenne pepper
2 T. garlic powder

Preheat oil to 350 degrees. Mix eggs, mustard and lemon in one bowl. Mix dry ingredients. Dip legs in egg mixture, roll in bread crumbs, coat well. Deep fry for 3 minutes or until dark golden brown.

Stephen Lee
New Orleans, Louisiana

Port Wine Sauce for Game

     currant jelly
     port wine
     stock
     salt
     lemon juice
  4 cloves
     cayenne

Simmer the cloves and stock together for ½ hour. Strain on the other ingredients and let all melt together. Part of the gravy from the game may be added to it.

Tanya Brown
Weston, Ohio

Beer Bread

Serves: several
Prep Time: several hours

  3 cups self-rising flour
  3 T. sugar
  1 12 oz. can beer (not lite)

Mix all ingredients together, knead, place in greased loaf pan and cover top of dough with soft margarine or butter flavored Crisco. Let rise. Bake at 350 degrees for 1 hour.

Robert Parker
Las Vegas, Nevada

Celebrity chefs

Pheasant and Cream

Serves: 4
Prep Time: 1½ hours

- **2 pheasants**
  flour
- **1 cup sour cream**
- **2 cups whole cream**
- **2 cups fresh mushrooms**

Bone pheasant breasts and legs. Flour meat pieces and brown lightly. Reduce heat, add sour cream, whole cream and fresh mushrooms. Simmer until very tender, approximately 1½ hours. Season to taste. Pour gravy over long grain rice.

Larry Anderson
Des Moines, Iowa

Larry Anderson
Wildlife Artist

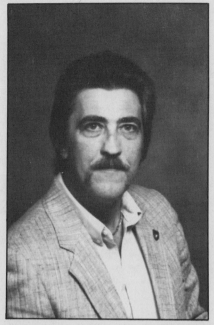

Scrunched down in a scrub oak blind waiting for a gobbler to work his way in, or sitting at an easel painting wildlife, Larry Anderson feels at home in either place. His accurate portrayals of the outdoors captures the realistic detail that can only be attained by an artist who is also a true sportsman.

When admiring a painting or drawing, it only takes an instant for the hunter/art lover to tell if the artist has really "been there." Larry Anderson has. His classrooms have been the timbers and lakes from Canada to Cuba. "Sometimes when I feel a bass pop my jig, or see a doe on a snowy hillside, I often forget I am fishing or hunting as I wonder how to work the scene out on canvas," says Larry.

Based with his family in Des Moines, Iowa, Larry travels extensively promoting his work and spending as much time in the field as he can. His talent and dedication have produced innumerable awards, and his work is regularly seen in dozens of magazines including *North American Hunter*. All of the pen & ink drawings in this *NAHC Wild Game Cookbook* are examples of Larry's fine and versatile work.

For more information on Larry Anderson's work and a list of the limited edition prints that he has available, write: *Larry Anderson, LDA Editions, 1603 Evans, Des Moines, IA 50315.*

Venison Roast/Stew

Serves: 4-6
Prep Time: 4 hours

3½ **lb. venison roast**
  4 **carrots**
  4 **potatoes**
  4 **onions**
  3 **cloves garlic**
  1 **stalk celery**
  1 **pkg. Lipton Onion Soup Mix**
  2 **sm. cans Hot V-8 Juice**
  2 **cups water**
    garlic powder
    onion powder
    mushrooms
    gravy thickener
    salt and pepper

Sprinkle roast with garlic and onion powder, then brown on both sides in hot oil. Place browned roast in oblong roasting pan. Put sliced onions and Lipton soup mix on top of roast with 2 cans Hot V-8 Juice. Add 1 cup water and celery. Cover with foil and bake at 350 degrees for 3 to 4 hours, until tender. The last hour add all remaining ingredients. Thicken drippings for gravy before serving.

Leland Clyde Brown, Jr.
Boca Raton, Florida

Leland C. Brown, Jr.
President
United States Products

As President of United States Products, Leland Brown, Jr. oversees the production of Gold Medallion, a bore cleaner and conditioner developed by shooting world-record holder Ferris Pindell which quickly and safely removes all fouling from any gun in less than 10 minutes.

The 50-year-old Brown is a busy man. In addition to his duties at United States Products, he is a mortgage broker, a member of the Boca Raton, Florida, Chamber of Commerce, a World Master Scuba Diver, a hydrospace submarine pilot and a member of numerous business associations. In his spare time he enjoys flying, squash racquets, sailing and bicycling.

Hunter's Stew

Serves: 6
Prep Time: 1 hour

- **2 lbs. venison, cubed**
- **½ lb. smoked sausage, sliced**
- **1 lg. onion, chopped**
- **½ cup celery, chopped**
- **2 28 oz. cans tomatoes**
- **1 can beer**
- **salt and pepper**
- **1 T. sugar**
- **1 tsp. rosemary**
- **1 tsp. basil**
- **2 lg. carrots, sliced**
- **2 lg. potatoes, cubed**

Brown venison and sausage in hot oil in Dutch oven. Add onion and celery and cook until tender. Add next 7 ingredients. Cover, reduce heat and simmer for ½ hour. Add carrots and potatoes and cook until vegetables are done. Serve with cornbread.

Jim Crumley
Roanoke, Virginia

Jim Crumley
President
Bowing Enterprises

Jim Crumley, the creator of Trebark camouflage, is a gifted innovator who has managed to combine his life-long passion for the outdoors and hunting with his industrial arts skills to revolutionize the way in which thousands of hunters now conceal themselves. Born and raised in Southern Virginia, Jim lives true to his heritage as demonstrated by his low-key business style and overall professional demeanor. Formally educated at Virginia Tech with significant experiences as a professional educator, Jim turned in his tutorial wares some 6 years ago to manage Bowing Enterprises, the parent company he began for his full line of Trebark products.

Having recently expanded his product line to include Trebark material in both khaki and sage coloration, Jim markets through his mail order catalog and a new retail outlet, Trebark Outfitters, in Roanoke, Virginia. His complete line of concealment material ranges from Trebark gloves to fully insulated and waterproof jackets, pants and boots to sportcoats. Through arrangements with numerous other top-of-the-line manufacturers, every conceivable hunting apparel and accessory item is now being offered in the Trebark pattern.

A well-rounded hunter and former guide, Jim has logged hundreds of miles in pursuit of whitetail deer and turkey. In addition, he is often on the trail in search of bear in Canada, boar in Florida, mulies and elk in Colorado, with bow in hand.

Chinese Fajita

Serves: 4
Prep Time: ½ hour

- **1 lb. elk steak, slightly frozen**
- **1 T. oil**
- **1 med. onion, thinly sliced**
- **1 lg. bell pepper, cut into ¼-inch slices**
  seasoned salt
  pepper
- **1 T. cooking sherry**
- **1 T. Worcestershire**
- **6 flour tortillas**
  sour cream, guacamole or salsa

Slice partially frozen steak diagonally across the grain into ¼-inch strips and set aside. Prepare vegetables and set aside. Coat wok with oil and heat to medium high (325 degrees) for 1 to 2 minutes. Add elk meat and stir fry until meat loses its pinkness, about 3 minutes. Add onions, green pepper and seasonings and stir fry until vegetables are crisp-tender, about 5 minutes. Scoop cooked mixture into tortillas. Top with sour cream, guacamole or salsa. Roll and serve.

Frank Dunkle
Washington, DC

Frank Dunkle
Director
U.S. Fish & Wildlife Service

Frank Dunkle has devoted his life to resource management for more than 40 years in the private, State and Federal sectors. Beginning as a special warden with the Montana Fish and Game Department while an undergraduate at Montana State University, he is now Director of the U.S. Fish and Wildlife Service. This Federal agency is responsible for our national program of fish and wildlife conservation.

Frank has served as director of Montana Department of Fish, Wildlife and Parks, executive director of the Montana Mining Association, and staff director of the Mountain Plains Federal Regional Council.

He also found time for politics, seeking the Republican gubernatorial nomination. He was elected to the Montana State Senate and was recognized as the Outstanding State Legislator of the Year in 1977 by the National Association of State and Federal Employees. In 1980 he served as executive director of the Montana State Republican Central Committee.

The Green Leaf Award from the Nature Conservancy, the Sears Foundation 1968 Water Conservation Award for Montana, and the 1971 American Motors National Conservation Award are among the awards Frank has received.

Charcoaled Dove

Serves: 2
Prep Time: 3 hours

4 dove breasts
1 cup salad oil
½ cup soy sauce
bacon slices
1 T. Worcestershire
1 cup vinegar
½ cup lemon juice
½ tsp. garlic salt

Mix oil, vinegar, soy sauce, Worcestershire, lemon juice and garlic salt in a glass bowl. Place dove breasts in the bowl and marinate at least 2 hours. Remove breasts from marinade and wrap each in ½ slice bacon secured with a toothpick. Cook over charcoal and baste often with the marinade. Grill approximately 10 minutes per side.

Bill Harper
Neosho, Missouri

Bill Harper
President
Lohman Manufacturing Co.

Bill Harper is President of Lohman Manufacturing Co., Inc. and has been an avid hunter for over 25 years. Bill has studied wildlife in its habitat, learning the languages and behavior of all kinds of game. He is a proficient guide, as well as an outstanding woodsman and conservationist. Bill believes hunting safety and good hunting practices ensure good hunting for all and for future generations.

Bill is a nationally-known lecturer and game calling expert and instructor. A winner of numerous championship calling contests, Bill has taught students who have gone on to win State, National and World Championships. Bill has been teaching the art of game calling since 1968 and sharing his hunting expertise with hunters throughout the nation. Several books on the subject of game calling have been authored by Bill Harper through the years.

Pheasant in Red Wine Sauce

Serves: 4
Prep Time: 1½ hour

  2 **pheasants, cut up**
  ½ **cup pancake mix**
  ½ **cup butter**
  2 **cups fresh mushrooms, sliced**
  1 **onion, chopped**
  2 **chicken bouillon cubes**
  1 **cup hot water**
    juice of ½ lemon
  1 **tsp. pepper**
  1 **tsp. salt**
  ¼ **cup dry red wine**

Roll pheasant in pancake mix. Saute in butter until brown.
Remove. Saute mushroom and onion in butter until brown.
Dissolve bouillon cube in 1 cup hot water. Replace pheasant
in skillet and add remaining ingredients, except wine.
Cover and cook over low heat for 1 hour or until tender. Stir
in dry red wine about 15 minutes before the end of the
cooking time.

Dave Perkins
Accokeek, Maryland

Dave Perkins
Nat'l. Marketing Manager
Beretta U.S.A.

Dave Perkins is the National Marketing Manager for Beretta U.S.A., and has been with the company for the last 5 years, having 18 years experience in the gun industry. Beretta U.S.A. is an affiliate of Beretta, Italy, but is a "made in the U.S.A." company that is incorporated in the United States. Beretta has recently won a $76 million contract to supply the U.S. Armed Forces with 320,000 9mm pistols.

Dave spends his days afield hunting birds, with pheasant being his favorite, and also enjoys skeet and sporting clays shooting. Dave has been a shotgunner since the age of 13 and also aims his guns at grouse, doves, Canada geese and woodcock.

Chianti Doves

Serves: 4-6
Prep Time: 1 hour

10 doves, either whole or halved
2 pkgs. dry spaghetti mix
butter
1 cup chicken broth
1 cup chianti wine

Pour 2 packages of spaghetti sauce mix into a plastic bag. Shake doves until well covered. Brown birds lightly in butter in frying pan. Add chicken broth and wine. Cover and simmer over low heat until tender, about ½ hour. Also can be done easily in a crockpot.

Daniel Poole
Washington, DC

Daniel A. Poole
Chairman of the Board
Wildlife Management Institute

Daniel A. Poole holds
wildlife degrees from the
University of Montana, and
has worked with the U.S.
Fish and Wildlife Service in
California and Utah and
with the Montana Fish,
Wildlife and Parks
Department. He joined the
Wildlife Management
Institute in Washington in
1952, rising to president of
the national, nonprofit
wildlife conservation group
in 1970 and board
chairman in 1987. Created by the sporting firearms and
ammunition manufacturers industry in 1911, the Institute
works to advance the restoration and scientific
management of wildlife through its Washington office and
field staffs. Its work is widely respected by Congress, federal
executive agencies, state wildlife departments and wildlife
professionals.

Pit Barbequed Javelina

Serves: several
Prep Time: overnight

- 1 **whole javelina, cleaned**
- 1 **onion, chopped**
- 7 **cloves garlic, chopped**
- 1 **cup Worcestershire**
- 2 **cups catsup**
- 2 **cups barbeque sauce**
- 7 **clove leaves**
  healthy shot of black pepper
  salt

Soak whole, cleaned javelina in salt water for a couple of hours before seasoning. Place javelina on ample piece of heavy duty aluminum foil and apply well-mixed ingredients on and around meat. Wrap securely in foil, possibly adding second sheet. Place into damp cloth baking bag. Place javelina in a pit where mesquite coals can be arranged below, around and above meat. Cover it with soil and allow to cook overnight or at least 7 to 9 hours. Meat will shred easily and is perfect for tacos and burritos.

Pete Shepley
Tucson, Arizona

Pete Shepley
President
Precision Shooting Equipment

Just a little more than 16 years ago, Pete Shepley was a full-time engineer for the Magnavox Corporation in Illinois. In his free time he dabbled with the designs of release aids, and later, compound bows.

Today Pete presides over Precision Shooting Equipment, or PSE, manufacturing compound bows, compound crossbows and archery accessories known around the world for their quality and dependability.

As one of North America's best known bowhunters, in the past 2 years he has successfully hunted grizzly, moose, barren ground caribou, black bear, yellowstone elk, cougar, stone sheep, desert bighorn sheep, whitetail deer and two species of wild turkey. But, as with most bowhunters who reside in the southwest, one of Pete's favorite game animals around his Tucson, Arizona home is the javelina.

"When the Good Lord decided to put the javelina in Arizona, he was thinking of the bowhunter," Pete says, "they are fun to hunt with a bow and arrow!"

Elk Pot Roast

Serves: 4
Prep Time: 1½ hours

  1 **4-5 pound elk roast**
     cooking oil
     salt and pepper
     onion slices
     potatoes
     carrots

Brown roast in oil on all sides in an 8-quart Dutch oven. Salt and pepper, add onion if desired. Cook browned roast over low heat for 2½ to 3 hours, turning every ½ hour. Add small amounts of water to prevent burning or sticking. Add potatoes and carrots and cook for 1 hour.

Gary Sutherland
Denver, Colorado

Gary Sutherland
Sales Manager
Redfield, Inc.

Redfield has been in business since 1909, manufacturing a complete line of sporting optical equipment; riflescopes, mounting systems, binoculars and spotting scopes. Their products are quality and are covered by a lifetime warranty. Over the years, Redfield has been responsible for many innovations in sights and riflescopes.

Gary has been with Redfield for a little over 6 years. For 2½ years he managed the Customer Service Department, and the remainder of the time he has been the National Sales Manager. Gary is married with two boys, ages 17 and 15 that are avid big game hunters. Living in Colorado, Gary and his family enjoy the things people move to Colorado for: hunting, fishing, camping and hiking.

SEND US YOUR GAME RECIPE

Title:_____

Serves:_____

Prep Time:_____

Ingredients:

_____
_____
_____
_____
_____
_____
_____
_____
_____

Directions:

_____ fold here
_____
_____
_____
_____
_____
_____
_____
_____
_____
_____
_____
_____
_____
_____
_____
_____
_____
_____
_____

Your NAHC Member#_____

Your Name_____

Address_____

City/State/Zip_____

North American Hunting Club
P.O. Box 35557
Minneapolis, MN 55435

SEND US YOUR GAME RECIPE

Title: _____

Serves: _____

Prep Time: _____

Ingredients:

_____
_____
_____
_____
_____
_____
_____
_____

Directions:

_____ fold
_____
_____
_____
_____
_____
_____
_____
_____
_____
_____
_____
_____
_____
_____
_____

Your NAHC Member # _____

Your Name _____

Address _____

City/State/Zip _____

A Great Gift Idea...
The NAHC Wild Game Cookbook!

Order extra copies of the 1988 Cookbook for
your friends and family. They make great gifts
– fun to read and practical as well!

You'll also like to have a second copy to keep
at the cabin or in with your camping gear.

Send your order in now and get yours at the
special Member's price of only $9.95 each.
(Non-members pay $14.95)

Send me ____ copies of the 1988 Wild Game Cookbook.
I'm enclosing $9.95 each (non-members pay $14.95).
Include $1.50 per order for Postage and Handling.

If paying by Check or Money Order, send this form in
an envelope with your payment to: NAHC Cookbook,
P.O. Box 35560, Minneapolis, MN 55435.
Charge customers may cut out this page, fold and mail.
(Don't forget to put on a stamp)

☐ Check here if you'd like to receive information about
ordering NAHC Wild Game Cookbooks from past years.

Payment Method:
___ Check or M.O.
___ MasterCard
___ Visa

Card # _____
Exp. Date _____
Signature _____

Name _____ Member # _____

Address _____

City/State/Zip _____

North American Hunting Club
P.O. Box 35560
Minneapolis, MN 55435

Hunters belong in the NAHC...
and it's so *simple* to join!
Cut out and mail one of the cards below.

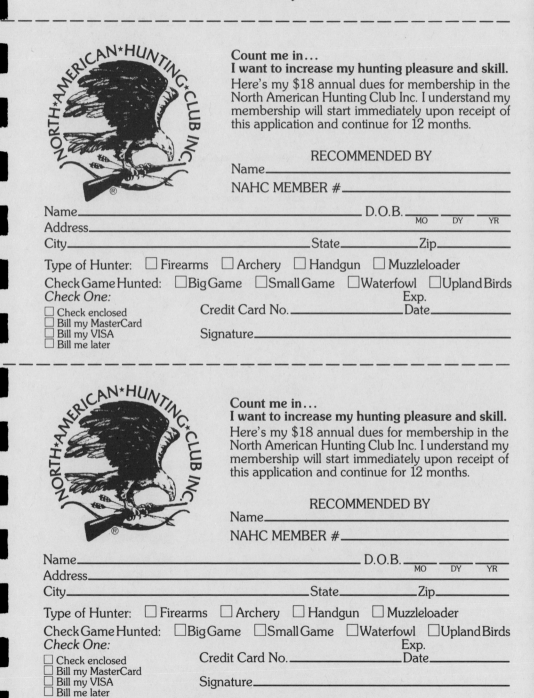

Count me in...
I want to increase my hunting pleasure and skill.

Here's my $18 annual dues for membership in the North American Hunting Club Inc. I understand my membership will start immediately upon receipt of this application and continue for 12 months.

RECOMMENDED BY

Name_____

NAHC MEMBER #_____

Name_____ D.O.B. ____ ____ ____
                                              MO   DY   YR
Address_____
City_____ State_____ Zip_____

Type of Hunter: ☐ Firearms ☐ Archery ☐ Handgun ☐ Muzzleloader
Check Game Hunted: ☐ Big Game ☐ Small Game ☐ Waterfowl ☐ Upland Birds
Check One:
☐ Check enclosed
☐ Bill my MasterCard   Credit Card No._____ Exp. Date_____
☐ Bill my VISA
☐ Bill me later   Signature_____

Count me in...
I want to increase my hunting pleasure and skill.

Here's my $18 annual dues for membership in the North American Hunting Club Inc. I understand my membership will start immediately upon receipt of this application and continue for 12 months.

RECOMMENDED BY

Name_____

NAHC MEMBER #_____

Name_____ D.O.B. ____ ____ ____
                                              MO   DY   YR
Address_____
City_____ State_____ Zip_____

Type of Hunter: ☐ Firearms ☐ Archery ☐ Handgun ☐ Muzzleloader
Check Game Hunted: ☐ Big Game ☐ Small Game ☐ Waterfowl ☐ Upland Birds
Check One:
☐ Check enclosed
☐ Bill my MasterCard   Credit Card No._____ Exp. Date_____
☐ Bill my VISA
☐ Bill me later   Signature_____

BUSINESS REPLY CARD
FIRST CLASS   PERMIT NO. 17619   MPLS., MN

POSTAGE WILL BE PAID BY ADDRESSEE

North American Hunting Club, Inc.
P.O. Box 35557
Minneapolis, Minn. 55435

BUSINESS REPLY CARD
FIRST CLASS   PERMIT NO. 17619   MPLS., MN

POSTAGE WILL BE PAID BY ADDRESSEE

North American Hunting Club, Inc.
P.O. Box 35557
Minneapolis, Minn. 55435

Index

caribou and moose, 101
  italian, 56
  moose, 95
mincemeat, 93
parmesan
  moose, 94
poontock, 65
potato chip, 89
roast
  dutch oven pot, 85
  elk pot, 176
  marinated, 86
  stew, 162
  swedish pot moose, 97
  tender, 82
sausage, 61
  ring bologna, 60
  stuffed mushrooms, 21
shish-ka-bobs, 90
sloppy joes, 17, 82
spaghetti squash with, 83
steaks, 62
  beer batter, 88
  chicken fried, 16
  marinated, 87
  strip filipino, 87
stew
  all-around, 55
  boxwood, 53
  cabbage patch, 103
  crockpot, 51, 52
  fruit, 23
  hunter's, 164
  moose, 101
  quick, 49
  roast, 162
stroganoff, 80, 81
  moose, 98

sweet and sour, 73
taco salad, 79
teriyaki, 75

WOODCOCK
Chablis, in, 27
Missouri, 138